FingerTales

Joan Hilyer Phelps

UpstartBooks

Fort Atkinson, Wisconsin

To my daughter, Hilery, who at age five told me,
"You and me, Mama, we can do anything!"
and to my husband, Barry, who agreed with her.

And, for my parents, Anne and Joe Hilyer,
who gave me my love for books.

Published by UpstartBooks
W5527 Highway 106
P.O. Box 800
Fort Atkinson, Wisconsin 53538-0800
1-800-448-4887

© Joan Hilyer Phelps, 2002
Cover design by Heidi Green, illustrations by Joan Hilyer Phelps

The paper used in this publication meets the minimum requirements of
American National Standard for Information Science —
Permanence of Paper for Printed Library Material. ANSI/NISO Z39.48-1992.

Contents

Introduction

A successful storytime is made up of several elements. At the core is quality literature that appeals to young children because of the illustrations as well as the text. Building on that, other elements you may choose to add consist of flannel board activities, songs, simple crafts and fingerplays, all of which are included in each theme-based chapter in this book. It is intended to help "storytellers" plan and execute an enjoyable and memorable storytime for the children attending.

Of the storytime elements mentioned, my favorites are the fingerplays and the puppets used to enhance them. They are the main focus of this book. Every attempt should be made to make the fingerplays you choose for storytime as appealing and delightful to see and hear as the picture books you are reading. We spend countless amounts of time searching for "the perfect books" to share with the children. We want the books to be almost magical for them! Why shouldn't we try to achieve the same magic with our fingerplays?

Choosing and Presenting Fingerplays

After you have chosen the appropriate books for your group (suggestions are included in each chapter), you're ready to "build" your storytime around them. Be as critical in choosing the fingerplays and other activities as you were in choosing the books. If you truly enjoy a fingerplay, your enthusiasm will be contagious.

After you have chosen fingerplays to share with the children, prepare a handout that includes all the fingerplays, songs, etc., you have planned and give one to each of the adults who will be attending. By doing this, you will have extra voices in addition to yours during your presentation, and the children will be more likely to participate. This will be a comfort to you during storytime, and later to the adults whose children will want to repeat the

rhymes when they return home. (You may also want to include a bibliography of the books you read.)

Making the Puppets

The patterns and instructions for the puppets are simple. Above all, use bright, pretty colors of felt and your puppets will capture the attention of your intended audience!

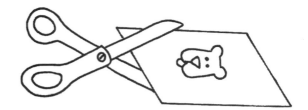

photocopy pattern and cut out

1. **First, photocopy the pattern and cut it out. You will use each pattern five times to make each set of puppets.**

- Tape each pattern piece in turn to an appropriate color of felt, covering the pattern completely. By doing this, the pattern cannot shift or move around while you're trying to cut it out. It will also protect your pattern from tearing, etc. You may notice your puppet patterns gradually getting larger from the build up of tape! This isn't necessarily a bad thing but to avoid it just make an effort to cut on the line each time. (A good pair of scissors will make this an easy task.)

- The Glove Puppets are the easiest, as they just require gluing Velcro to the backs after they have been assembled. The Finger Puppets require some thought, but just a little!

- Felt is great to work with because it will stretch a little if needed, but if you think the puppets may be a little too small or large, adjust the size accordingly on the copier.

- Remember that you'll always need to cut *two* of the main body of the puppet from felt.

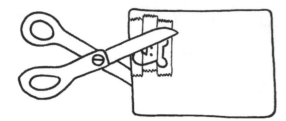

tape pattern to felt and cut out

2. After the rest of the pieces are cut out, assemble the front of the puppet as if you were making it for use on a glove.

glue puppet pieces together
with hot glue

3. Next place the completed front onto the back and glue them together using as thin a line of glue as possible around the edges, only leaving the bottom open for your finger. If the puppet has arms, glue the arm piece across the back now.

finish details with
a fine-tipped,
permanent marker

4. Finish any details on the puppets with a fine-tipped permanent marker. Drawing on felt or any "fuzzy" surface can be tricky. Instead of using regular strokes, try drawing a series of connecting dots. You'll have crisper lines on the puppets with this method.

Making Puppet Gloves

You can use any glove for your puppets but why not enhance the visual appeal even more by making your gloves as unique as possible? Using the pattern provided on pg. 8, make several from bright, vivid colors of felt that will complement different puppets and palm props.

1. They are simple to make using a hot-glue gun.

- Staple two pieces of felt together so the two halves will match perfectly.

- Next, tape the pattern to the felt and cut it out, again using a good pair of scissors.

- Using your glue gun, work in short sections making as thin a line of glue as possible and carefully pressing it down as you go to seal the edges.

- Remember to leave bottom open for your hand.

- Glue Velcro to the fingertips of both sides and the palm area so you won't be limited to which hand you can wear it on.

- It is also nice to use the Velcro strips designed to be used as tie wraps for computer cables as they come in a package of five assorted bright colors that are easy to match to the colors of felt.

- If the Velcro is the same color as the glove it won't be distracting when a puppet is removed.

3. As you can tell from the pattern, the fingers of the glove seem a bit wide.

- By making them that way you transform the glove into a miniature flannel board. (All of the puppets in this book can easily be used on a flannel board by simply enlarging them on the copier.)

- The glove gives you the convenience of having an activity literally at your fingertips without having to transport and set up a large board, which is very appealing if you travel to schools, day-cares, library branches, etc.

Scenery Gloves

Now here's the fun part! Because felt gloves are so easy to make, you can fashion "scenery" gloves that will enhance the appearance of your puppets even more and will keep even a very young audience's attention. In addition to solid colors, design gloves that provide a backdrop for the characters and help them tell the story in the fingerplay.

Make a **tree glove**, as shown, for fingerplays such as "5 Little Monkeys Swinging in a Tree" and "Way Up High in the Apple Tree." This is simply done by making a glove from brown felt, extending its length to the middle of your forearm and gluing several green felt leaves to each fingertip. (Gluing leaves to the front and the back of each fingertip will give the tree both fullness and dimension.)

A **sky blue glove with white felt clouds** works for "sky" fingerplays such as "5 Little Kites."

A **black glove with small white stars** works for "5 Little Aliens," "5 Little Fireflies" and "5 Little Stars" and other "nighttime" fingerplays.

A **glove with a castle scene** would make the perfect backdrop for fingerplays with a fairy tale theme and so on.

You can also allow your scenery gloves to pull double duty by using a solid color on the reverse side.

Making the puppets, gloves, flannel board characters, etc., included in this book can be a very enjoyable activity. As you make them, add your own personal touches and details that will make them uniquely yours. The return on the time spent will be many delighted children at your storytime for years to come!

Glove Pattern

Enlarge pattern and extend to desired length.

Glove Puppets

Aliens

Take Me to Your Leader!

Fingerplay: 5 Little Aliens

5 (4,3,2) little aliens
Came down from outer space.
Each had antennas *(Touch head.)*
And purple spots on their face. *(Touch face.)*
One little alien
Continued on his trip
And jumped into his spaceship
And took off with a zip!
(Quickly remove one alien and "blast" him away!)

<u>Closing Verse</u>
1 little alien
Came down from outer space.
He had antennas
And purple spots on his face.
The last little alien
Then continued on his trip
And jumped into his spaceship
And took off with a zip!

Puppet & Palm Patterns

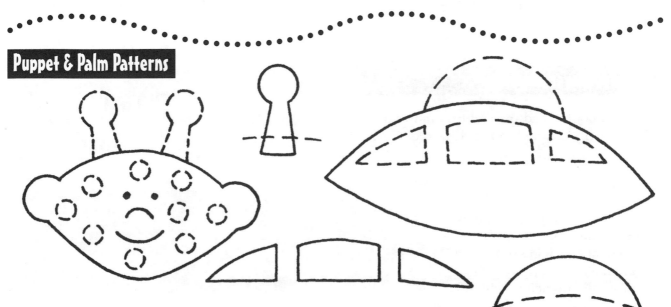

Hint: When making these puppets, it may be less time-consuming to paint the spots on the faces with fabric paint instead of using felt. Personally, I prefer the felt, but using hot glue on such tiny pieces can be risky! Either way, use whatever color of felt or paint you have and just change the color mentioned in the fingerplay to suit.

Suggested Books to Share

McNaughton, Colin. *Here Come the Aliens.* Candlewick Press, 1995. A rhyming text about not-so-nice aliens who are on their way to earth. Each page describes a creature aboard the spacecraft and ends with the line "the aliens are coming," which provides the opportunity for the children to participate by chanting that line with you throughout the book.

Ottley, Matt. *What Faust Saw.* Dutton Children's Books, 1996. When Faust does his job as the family's watchdog and barks at the aliens he sees outside, the family fusses at him and puts him out! Feeling unappreciated, Faust runs away.

Wiesner, David. *June 29, 1999.* Clarion, 1992. A third grader named Holly sends her science experiment consisting of vegetable seedlings off into space on May 11, 1999. On June 29, gigantic vegetables start appearing in the sky. Is it Holly's experiment or the work of aliens? As expected, David Wiesner's pictures are fantastic!

Props: Planet & Stars

Make construction paper planets and stars to suspend from the ceiling or hang on the walls. Use fishing line if possible and hang them so low as to be just above the children's heads. This will give the feeling of being among the planets in space!

Activity: Movement Chant

Between books, lead the children in this movement activity chanted to the rhythm of "Teddy Bear, Teddy Bear."

Alien, Alien
Alien, alien turn around.
Alien, alien hop up and down.
Alien, alien stand on your toes.
Alien, alien wiggle your nose.
Alien, alien jump up high.
Alien, alien reach for the sky.
Alien, alien run in place.
Alien, alien blast off to space!
(Put hands above head with fingers touching, forming a rocket shape, and jump!)

Take Home: Alien Headbands

Materials Needed
- Tagboard strips
- Pom-poms
- Pipe cleaners
- Tape
- Crayons

Prior to storytime, hot glue pom-poms to pipe cleaners and cut strips for headbands. Mix and match colors of pom-poms and pipe cleaners. The more colors, the better the children will like them. Have children color the headbands, then assist them with sizing them to their heads and secure with tape. Let children choose two antennas and tape them to the headband. See illustration below for for finished project.

Alligators

Snap!

Fingerplay: 5 Little Alligators

1 (2,3,4) little alligator(s)
Having a party in the swamp.
Is (are) joined by another one
Watch them dance and romp!

<u>Closing Verse</u>
5 little alligators
Down in the swamp.
Having an alligator party
Watch them dance and romp!

Puppet Pattern

Hint: Make the teeth for your alligators by cutting a thin strip of white felt with your pinking shears on one edge. Cut two pieces to the length needed for the top and lower teeth and glue to the back side of the puppet's mouth. Add the pupil with a fine-tipped permanent marker.

Suggested Books to Share

Hurd, Thacher. *Mama Don't Allow: Starring Miles and the Swamp Band*. Harper, 1984. When Miles and his band get a "gig" playing at the alligators' ball they end up having to outsmart their host when the dance is over and it's time to eat. Especially when it looks like the band is on the menu!

Mayer, Mercer. *There's an Alligator Under my Bed*. Dial, 1987. A little boy finds a way to lure the alligator under his bed out to the garage.

Sendak, Maurice. *Alligators All Around*. Harper & Row, 1962. A family of alligators makes their way through the alphabet "ordering oatmeal," "wearing wigs," "yackety-yacking," etc.

Props: Planet & Stars

I was fortunate to have the ultimate prop for the book *Mama Don't Allow* when two good friends who are musicians played the banjo and guitar while I read. Thacher Hurd has included the music for the song by the same name in this delightful book. If you are as lucky as I am and have such talented friends, the children will be thrilled with your presentation. If musicians are not available, prerecorded music would be the next best thing. I have used this method also with good results.

Activity: Flannel Board

Using the patterns provided on pg. 15, make the characters for the traditional fingerplay "5 Little Monkeys" for your flannel board. Substitute an alligator puppet for the pattern if you have one. If not, cut out two alligators from the pattern, hot glue together and mount on a dowel so that you can "creep" the alligator toward the monkeys. Make a simple tree from felt for the monkeys to swing from as shown in the illustration for setting up your flannel board.

5 Little Monkeys

5 (4,3,2,1) little monkeys
Swinging in a tree
Teasing Mr. Alligator,
Can't catch me!" *(Teasingly.)*
Along comes Mr. Alligator
As - sly - as - he - can - be *(Whisper slowly.)*
Gotcha!
(Loudly while snatching one monkey off the board!)

Take Home: Clothespin Alligators

Materials Needed

* Clothespins
* Photocopies of alligator "parts" on tagboard
* Green crayons or markers
* Tape or glue sticks

Prior to Storytime, photocopy the patterns for the alligator provided. Since the parts are small, just use one photocopy as a pattern and cut several at a time. Stapling several sheets of paper together and tracing your pattern onto the top sheet easily does this. It will save you some time if you snip the "toes" of the alligator with your pinking shears instead of using conventional scissors for such detailed cuts. Add the pupils to the eyes with a fine-tipped marker. Have the children color their clothespins and the other parts. Fold the eyepiece on the dotted lines and tape or glue the legs and eyes to the clothespin as shown in the picture. The alligators can be "snapped" onto the children's clothes or books!

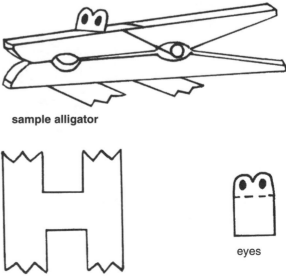

sample alligator

feet

eyes

Flannel Board Patterns

Enlarge patterns to desired size.

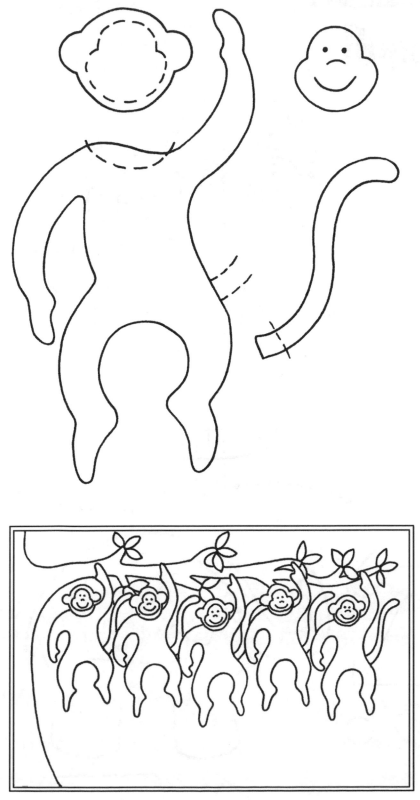

sample flannel board

Circus

Clowning Around!

Fingerplay: 5 Funny Clowns

5 (4,3,2) funny clowns
Standing on their toes.
Each with a hat
And a big red nose.
Along came an elephant
In the parade,
And 1 funny clown
Rode away!

Closing Verse
1 funny clown
Standing on his toes.
He had a hat
And a big red nose.
Along came an elephant
In the parade,
And the last funny clown
Rode away!

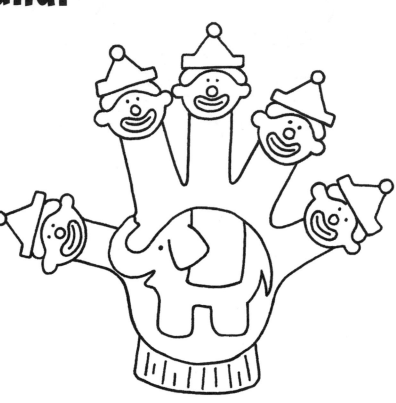

Puppet & Palm Patterns

Hint: Assemble puppets as shown. Use the round shape for the nose and the ball on top of the hat. Use lots of different, bright colors to make the puppets. The eyes and the detail on the mouth are done with a fine-tipped permanent marker. Attach Velcro to the back of the clowns and the elephant palm prop.

Suggested Books to Share

Campbell Ernst, Lisa. *Ginger Jumps*. Bradbury Press, 1990. Ginger is a dog who lives with the circus but dreams of living with a human family. While practicing a new circus act, in which she must jump from a platform into the arms of a clown, she realizes the little clown is really a little girl and hopes this could be her chance at having a family to belong to.

Emberley, Rebecca. *My Mother's Secret Life*. Little, Brown & Co., 1998. A little girl can't believe her mother does anything but take care of her until she dreams she sees her mother flying on a trapeze at the circus!

McGuirk, Leslie. *Tucker Over the Top*. Dutton, 2000. Tucker the terrier is off to the circus where he sees all kinds of animals performing and is recruited to use his skateboarding skills in an act himself!

Falconer, Ian. *Olivia Saves the Circus*. Atheneum, 2001. The circus performers were out sick. "Luckily I knew how to do everything," Olivia the feisty young pig says. She confidently tells the story of how she rode a unicycle, tamed lions, flew through the air and more.

Props: Circus Big Top

Give your storytime room a real circus feeling by hanging crepe paper streamers from the ceiling. Starting from the center of the room, attach streamers to the ceiling and drape them out to the top of the walls. Use bright, alternating colors to achieve a "big top" atmosphere. Use colored tape to make three large circles on the floor, and bring in all your stuffed animals!

Activity: Face Painting

Recruit help for this one! Ask a co-worker, "Friends Of The Library" member or storytime parents to help you with face painting. Let the children choose from simple circus symbols such as a balloon, cotton candy cone or a big red dot on their nose like a clown. Let the children waiting to have their faces painted play in the "three-ringed circus" you have set up with the stuffed animals.

Take Home: Clown Hats & Clown Shoes

If you have time for both of these projects you'll end up with a room full of the cutest clowns around!

Clown Hats—Materials Needed

- Tagboard
- Tape
- Crayons or markers
- Yarn
- Hole puncher

Prior to storytime, cut out cone shapes for clown hats. I have included a pattern on pg. 18, but the dotted line must be put on the fold of a large sheet of paper to make the hat large enough to use. Have children color their hats then shape them into cones and secure with tape. Punch two holes on both sides and tie yarn that can be used to tie under the children's chins to secure the hats on them.

Clown Shoes—Materials Needed

- Shoe pattern
- Construction paper
- Crayons
- Tape

Enlarge the shoe pattern on pg. 18 to the appropriate size for your age group. For little ones, don't make it so large that it will interfere with their walking ability and cause tripping. Cut out enough shoes for two per child. Have children color two shoes and assist them in taping them around their ankles.

Clown Hat Pattern

Enlarge pattern to desired size.

Clown Shoe Pattern

Enlarge pattern to desired size.

Cookies

Yum, Yum!

Fingerplay: 5 Yummy Cookies

5 (4,3,2) yummy cookies
All chocolate chip.
Were sitting in the cookie jar
When the table tipped!
The cookie jar tumbled,
1 cookie crumbled. *(Remove one cookie.)*
How many cookies are left?
(Pause for reply from children.)

<u>Closing Verse</u>
1 yummy cookie
It was chocolate chip.
Was sitting in the cookie jar
When the table tipped!
The cookie jar tumbled,
1 cookie crumbled. *(Remove last cookie.)*
How many cookies are left?
(Pause for reply from children.)

Puppet & Palm Patterns

Hint: Use light brown felt for the cookies and dark brown for the chips. These can be cut freehand without using the pattern to give them an authentic cookie appearance. The same with the chips. Vary the placement of the chips from cookie to cookie. On the palm prop, use a permanent marker to label the cookie jar, then attach Velcro to the cookies and the palm prop.

Suggested Books to Share

Aylesworth, Jim. *Old Black Fly.* Holt, 1992. A fly bothers a whole alphabet of items including cookies. The book also gives the children a "release" by letting them chant "Shoo fly! Shoo fly! Shoo!" throughout the story.

Hutchins, Pat. *The Doorbell Rang.* Greenwillow Books, 1986. Each time the doorbell rings, it brings more friends to share the cookies that have just been baked.

Joffe Numeroff. Laura. *If You Give a Mouse a Cookie.* Harper, 1985. One request after another leaves a little boy exhausted at the end of his day with a mouse.

Lass, Bonnie and Philemon Sturges. *Who Took the Cookies from the Cookie Jar?* Little, Brown & Company, 2000. A skunk follows a trail of crumbs as he questions an assortment of desert animals as to who stole the cookies. The authors have included the music to the song in their book.

Props: Doorbell

This is one of my favorite props for storytime. Prior to reading *The Doorbell Rang*, purchase an inexpensive, wireless doorbell system and place the bell in a hidden spot in the room within its range. Using removable tape, secure the button that operates the bell to the back of the book where it can be easily pushed with your thumb while remaining undetected by the children. The text will cue you as to when to ring the doorbell. It will be well worth your investment when you see the excitement it brings to your little listeners.

Activity: Flannel Board

Using the patterns provided on pgs. 21 and 22, make the figures to use on the flannel board while reciting "Who Took the Cookie." Substitute the animals' sounds for the traditional reply of "who me?" Prior to storytime, conceal a felt cookie behind the animal of your choice. Attach the cookie with a small piece of Velcro to the back of the animal. Have the children name the animals and chant

along with you. Finish the activity with a guessing game as to whom the real "culprit" is by turning over each animal (saving the "guilty" one until last). These flannel board figures can also be used with many other stories including "The Gingerbread Man."

Who Took the Cookie from the Cookie Jar?

Who took the cookie from the cookie jar?
Horse *(Point to animal.)* took the cookie from the cookie jar!
Neigh, neigh?
Yes, you!
Couldn't be!
Then, who?

Proceed with remaining animals and their sounds: Cat—meow, meow; Dog—woof, woof; Cow—moo, moo; Pig—oink, oink.

Take Home: Cookie Jar

Materials Needed

- Photocopies of cookie jar
- Crayons
- Tape
- Cookies

Photocopy a cookie jar on pg. 22 for each child, making sure the jar is on the far right side of an 8.5" x 11" sheet of paper. Let children color the cookie jar and then fold the paper in half. Let children tape the bottom and side closed, leaving the top open and forming a pocket. As the children leave storytime, offer each a cookie to put in their "cookie jar."

Flannel Board Patterns

Enlarge patterns to desired size.

Flannel Board Patterns, continued

Enlarge pattern to desired size.

Cookie Jar Pattern

This is a good size for the craft.

Fireflies

Night Lights

Fingerplay: 5 Little Fireflies

1 (2,3,4) little firefly
Flashing in the night.
Blink, blink, blink, blink
(Wiggle fingers in rhythm.)
Watch it (them) shine so bright.
Here comes another one
(Add one puppet.)
With its (their) flashing light(s)!

Closing Verse
5 little fireflies
Flashing in the night.
Blink, blink, blink, blink
(Wiggle fingers in rhythm.)
What a beautiful sight!

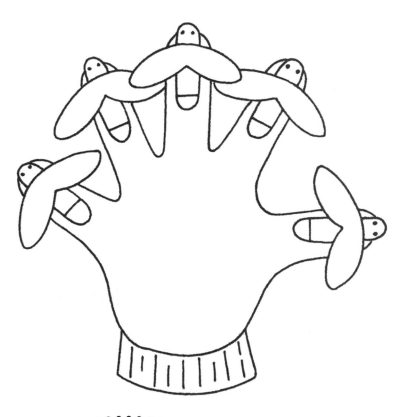

Puppet Patterns

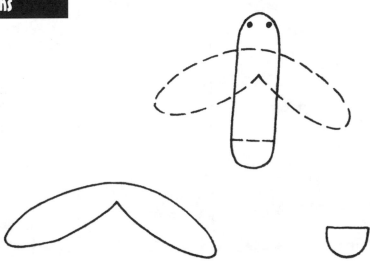

Hint: Use green felt for the body of the fireflies, yellow for the lights and white for the wings. Assemble as shown, and glue Velcro to the backs.

Suggested Books to Share

Brinckloe, Julie. *Fireflies!* MacMillian, 1985. A little boy captures a jar full of fireflies but has second thoughts about keeping them when their lights start to grow dim.

Carle, Eric. *The Very Lonely Firefly.* Philomel Books, 1995. A lonely firefly's search for another firefly leads him to an assortment of different lights before he finally finds a group of fireflies with real flashing lights.

Eastman, P. D. *Sam and the Firefly.* Beginner Books, 1958. The firefly in this story is a very talented skywriter but his talent isn't appreciated by all!

Sturges, Philemon. *Ten Flashing Fireflies.* North-South Books, 1995. A counting book.

Waber, Bernard. *A Firefly Named Torchy.* Houghton Mifflin, 1970. A little firefly is unhappy because his light is too bright.

Props: Blinking "Fireflies"

Since it would be impossible to have real fireflies visit during storytime, do the next best thing. Simulate the attraction we have to them by stringing small, blinking, white holiday lights around the room. Dim the lights if possible.

Activity: Movement Chant

Lead children in the following activity. Have them wiggle their fingers as if their fingers are little fireflies blinking.

Blinking Fireflies

(To the tune of "Twinkle, Twinkle Little Star")

Blinking, blinking fireflies bright
(Wiggle fingers all around.)

Blinking, blinking through the night.

Blink on my head, and blink on my toes
(Wiggle fingers on head then toes.)

Blink on my knees, and blink on my nose.
(Wiggle fingers on knees then nose.)

Blinking, blinking fireflies bright
(Wiggle fingers all around.)

Blinking, blinking through the night.

Take Home: Glow-in-the-Dark Fireflies

Materials Needed

- Photocopies of firefly
- Paper brads
- Crayons
- Glow-in-the-dark stickers

Enlarge the patterns below to the desired size. Photocopy a set of firefly pieces for each child. (Be sure to make two wings per firefly.) Cut pieces out ahead of time, and punch out holes where indicated. Have children color pieces. Demonstrate how to assemble wings to body. Give children a glow-in-the-dark sticker to put on their firefly. Explain how the sticker will glow in a dark room.

sample fireflies (sticker is placed on "tail")

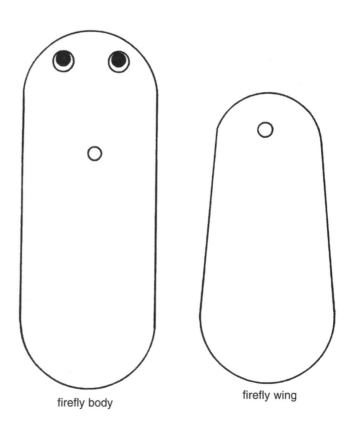

firefly body   firefly wing

Gingerbread Men

Run, Run as Fast as You Can!

Fingerplay: 5 Little Gingerbread Men

5 (4, 3, 2) little gingerbread men
In the oven baking.
5 little gingerbread men
In the oven mischief-making!
Lets peek inside
To see if they're done.
Out one jumps,
And away he runs! *(Remove one puppet.)*

Closing Verse
1 little gingerbread man
In the oven baking.
1 little gingerbread man
In the oven mischief-making!
Lets peek inside
To see if he's done.
Out he jumps,
And away he runs! *(Remove last puppet.)*

Puppet & Palm Patterns

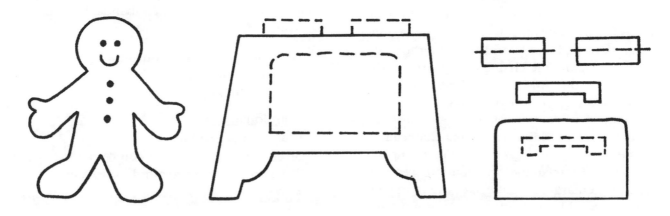

Hint: These puppets can be decorated in several different ways. You can use tiny rickrack at the wrists and ankles or fabric paint. Finish the faces with a fine-tipped permanent maker, and hot glue Velcro to the backs.

Suggested Books to Share

Brett, Jan. *The Gingerbread Baby.* Putnam, 1999. A mother and son bake a gingerbread baby that escapes from the oven and leads a chase similar to that in the classic.

Galdone, Paul. *The Gingerbread Boy.* Seabury Press, 1975. A retelling of the classic story with illustrations by the author.

Ginsburg, Mirra. *The Clay Boy.* Greenwillow Books, 1997. A retelling of a Russian folktale in which a couple makes a son out of clay who has such a huge appetite that he eats everything in his path.

Props: Gingerbread Man "Mascot"

Make a gingerbread man from felt. Enlarge the pattern on pg. 27 to the size you wish and cut two from light brown felt. Glue the seams together with hot glue, leaving a section open for stuffing. Stuff with fiberfill and finish gluing closed. Decorate with white rickrack by hot gluing it at wrist and ankles. Complete the face with pom-pom features and/or permanent markers. Make the gingerbread man your mascot for this storytime.

Activity: Flannel Board

The classic story of the gingerbread man is a wonderful flannel board story. If presented this way instead of being read, it also allows a greater opportunity for the children to participate in the story. Everyone loves to chant "run, run as fast as you can. You can't catch me, I'm the gingerbread man!" And it is easier to repeatedly name the characters involved in the chase if they are displayed on the flannel board. Use the patterns provided on pgs. 27 and 28 to make the four main characters of the story. The patterns for the additional animal characters can be found in the "Cookie" chapter on pgs. 21 and 22. To make the presentation even more attractive, enlarge the pattern of the oven palm prop to use with the story so that it is more in scale with the rest of the characters. If you don't glue the door onto the oven you could place the gingerbread man "inside" and then let him "jump" out to make his escape!

Take Home: Gingerbread Man Headbands

Materials Needed

- Photocopies of gingerbread man
- Paper strips for headbands
- Crayons
- Tape

Cut out gingerbread men and headband strips prior to storytime. Have children color a gingerbread man and headband. Assist them in sizing the headband to fit and secure with tape. Finish by letting each child tape the gingerbread man to the headband. See pg. 28 for pattern.

Activity: Final Movement Chant

After the children finish making their headbands as described in the "Take Home" activity, it's fun to bring them together as a group before they leave for this activity. With everyone wearing his or her headbands, lead the activity as follows. Begin with:

Hop, hop, as high as you can!
You can't catch me,
I'm the gingerbread man!

Additional Verses
Clap, clap, as soft as you can!
Stretch, stretch as tall as you can!
Turn around, turn around as slow, etc.

End with
Wave good-bye as nice as you can!
I'll see you next week,
At storytime again!

Enlarge patterns to desired size. See next page for additional pattern.

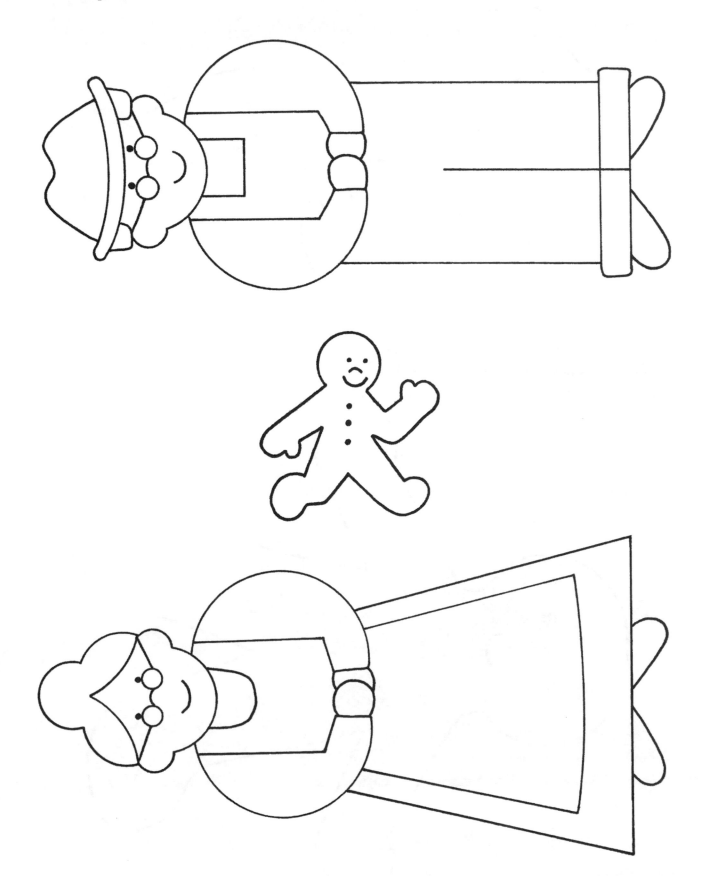

Flannel Board Patterns, continued

Gingerbread Man Headband Pattern

This pattern is also used for the gingerbread man mascot.

Leprechauns

Lucky Leprechauns

Fingerplay: 5 Lucky Leprechauns

5 (4,3,2) lucky leprechauns
Standing in a row.
Dressed in green
From head to toe!
One lucky leprechaun
Was afraid their secret
Would be told
So he slid down the rainbow
(Remove one leprechaun.)
To guard their pot of gold!

<u>Closing Verse</u>
1 lucky leprechaun
Standing in a row.
Dressed in green
From head to toe!
The last lucky leprechaun
Was afraid their secret
Would be told
So he slid down the rainbow
(Remove last leprechaun.)
To guard their pot of gold!

Puppet & Palm Patterns

Hint: Assemble puppets using the dotted lines as guides. Use orange felt for the beards and complete the faces with a permanent marker. Attach Velcro to the back of each puppet.

Suggested Books to Share

Balian, Lorna. *Leprechauns Never Lie.* Abingdon, 1980. Ninny Nanny catches a leprechaun who tricks her into doing her chores as she searches for his pot of gold.

Bunting, Eve. *St. Patrick's Day in the Morning.* Houghton Mifflin, 1980. Jamie tries to find a way to prove he's not too young to march in the parade.

De Paola, Tomie. *Jamie O'Rourke and the Big Potato.* G.P. Putnam's Sons, 1992. Jamie is the laziest man in Ireland. When he catches a leprechaun, Jamie lets the leprechaun give him seed for the biggest potato ever instead of gold. That way, he'll never have to garden again.

McDermott, Gerald. *Tim O'Toole and the Wee Folk.* Viking Penguin, 1990. Tim is given magical items by the wee folk, only to have them taken from him by a couple named McGoon.

Tucker, Kathy. *Leprechaun in the Basement.* Whitman, 1999. A young boy discovers a leprechaun living in his basement. He tries to convince the leprechaun to help his family through the rough time they're having since his father lost his job.

Props: Plenty 'O Green

Use shamrocks, rainbow pictures and anything green to decorate your storytime area for St. Patrick's Day.

Activity: Gold Coin Hunt

Prior to storytime, hide chocolate coins wrapped in gold foil in your storytime area. Choose a time best suited for your particular group, whether it is in the middle or end of your storytime, and let the children "hunt for gold!"

Take Home: Leprechaun Finger Puppets

Materials Needed

- Photocopies of puppet
- Crayons

Photocopy and cut out one puppet below for each child. Also cut out the finger holes indicated by the dotted lines. Let children color the puppets. Demonstrate how to use them.

finger puppet pattern

Lions

King of the Jungle

Fingerplay: 5 Ferocious Lions

Deep in the jungle
What did I hear?
5 (4,3,2) ferocious lions
Roaring loud and clear.
"Roar" said the lions, *(Roar loudly.)*
"Scat!" said I *(Say "scat" loudly.)*
And one ferocious lion
Ran away. Good-bye!

<u>Closing Verse</u>
Deep in the jungle
What did I hear?
1 ferocious lion
Roaring loud and clear.
"Roar" said the lion, *(Roar loudly.)*
"Scat!" said I *(Say "scat" loudly.)*
And the last ferocious lion
Ran away. Good-bye!

Palm & Puppet Patterns

See next page for puppet patterns.

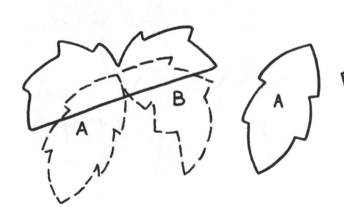

Palm Prop Patterns

Hint: These puppets are simple and large enough to wear directly on your fingers instead of a glove if you prefer. Just cut two manes instead of one and glue them together, leaving an area at the bottom open for your finger. Then complete the puppet as you would for a glove by gluing on the tongue, then the face, then the nose. Draw the eyes on with a permanent marker. If you make the glove puppets, don't forget to glue Velcro to the backs.

Suggested Books to Share

Axtell, David. *We're Going on a Lion Hunt.* Henry Holt and Co., 2000. Two brave sisters encounter many obstacles on their lion hunt before they meet up with one and hurriedly backtrack to the safety of their home.

Demarest, Chris L. *Clemens' Kingdom.* Lothrop, Lee and Shepard, 1983. Clemens, the lion, decides to leave his post outside the library to explore all the wonders inside.

Newberry, Clare Turlay. *Herbert the Lion.* Smithmark, 1998. A young girl is given a lion cub as a gift from her mother, but as he grows, his size begins to frighten people who don't know him, forcing the family to find him a new home.

Sendak, Maurice. *Pierre: A Cautionary Tale in Five Chapters and a Prologue.* Harper, 1962. Pierre's only reply is "I don't care" until he changes his attitude after he meets a hungry lion.

Wells, Rosemary. *A Lion for Lewis.* Dial Press, 1982. While playing with his siblings, Lewis is unhappy with the roles he is given in their pretend play until he discovers a lion suit in the corner of the attic.

Props: Lion Puppet

If you don't have a lion puppet to use for this storytime, you can easily make one using the basic hand puppet pattern provided on pg. 34. Extend the length of the puppet pattern by at least three inches at the dotted line. Cut two from brown felt and glue them together, leaving the bottom open for your hand. Next, enlarge the lion face and mane finger puppet patterns until they are the appropriate scale to fit the hand puppet, assemble the parts and then hot glue them to the hand puppet. A tail and paw prints may be added to the puppet if you like.

Activity: Movement Chant

Play a lion version of "Going On a Bear Hunt." Have children sit on the floor with legs crossed. Alternate patting legs as if walking while chanting the following:

Going on a Lion Hunt

Going on a lion hunt
Going on a lion hunt
What do I see?
What do I see?
I see a <u>field of grass</u>!
Can't go around it!
Can't go over it!
Gotta go through it!
<u>Whoosh, whoosh, whoosh, whoosh, whoosh.</u>

Substitute underlined items with other obstacles and the appropriate sound effects that you might encounter on a lion hunt. On the closing verse, arrive at the lion's den, see the lion and run rapidly by patting knees as you backtrack back through the obstacles you had encountered. Finish by seeing your house, running inside, closing the door and locking it safely behind you. Invite and encourage the children to help think of different obstacles. It will only add to the fun of this activity.

Take Home: Clothespin Lions

<u>Materials Needed</u>

- Photocopies of lion
- Crayons
- Clothespins (two per child)
- Yarn

Prior to storytime, make copies of the lion below (preferably from tagboard), cut them out and punch out holes for the tails where shown. Have children color the lions and the clothespins. Demonstrate clipping the clothespins on for legs. Assist them with tying yarn on for tails. The lions will stand if clothespins are spaced properly.

Basic Hand Puppet Pattern

Enlarge pattern to desired size.

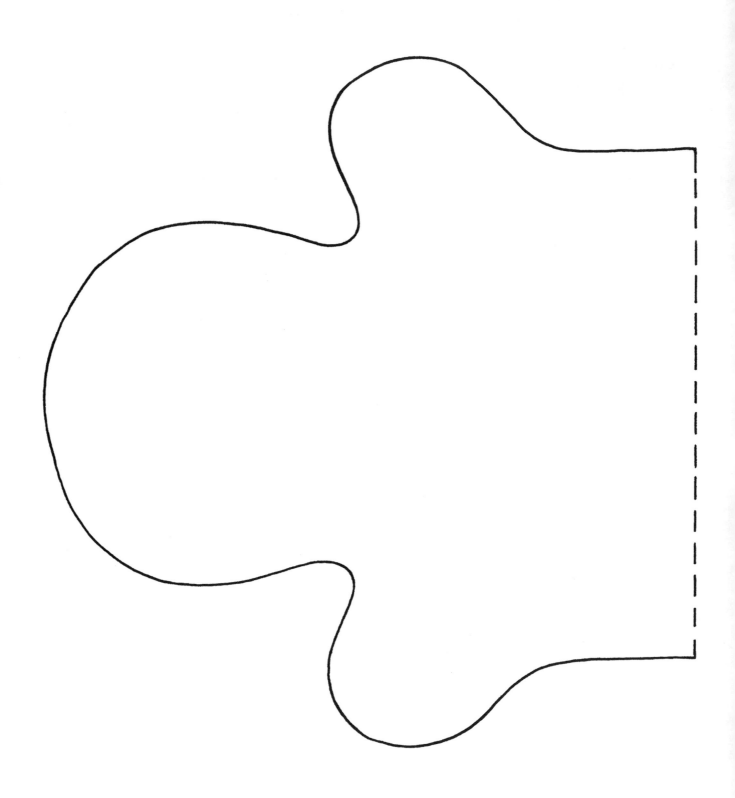

Pigs

Oink!

Fingerplay: 5 Little Pigs

5 (4,3,2) little pigs
Having so much fun.
Rolling in the mud,
And sleeping in the sun.
Here comes the farmer
Bringing corn by the bunch.
Away one pig runs *(Remove one pig.)*
To the trough for its lunch!

<u>Closing Verse</u>
1 little pig
Having so much fun.
Rolling in the mud,
And sleeping in the sun.
Here comes the farmer
Bringing corn by the bunch.
Away the last pig runs *(Remove last pig.)*
To the trough for its lunch!

Puppet Patterns

Hint: Assemble as shown using the dotted lines as guides. Hot glue the tail to the pig's back, twist it to the front, and tack it down with a little glue to form a kink. Glue Velcro to the back.

Suggested Books to Share

Christelow, Eileen. *The Great Pig Search.* Clarion, 2001. Bert and Ethel go to Florida to look for their runaway pigs and find them in unexpected places.

Falconer, Ian. *Olivia.* Simon and Schuster, 2000. Olivia fills her day with trips to the beach and the museum, moving the cat, daydreaming and wearing both she and her mother out!

Lester, Helen. *Me First.* Houghton Mifflin, 1992. Being first is very important to Pinkerton the pig but it also gets him into trouble!

Most, Bernard. *Z-Z-Zoink!* Harcourt Brace, 1999. A little pig snores so loudly that none of the barnyard animals will let him sleep with them.

Numeroff, Laura. *If You Give a Pig a Pancake.* HarperCollins, 1998. A sequence of events starts by giving a pig a pancake.

Props: Pig Snout

Make a pig snout to wear when introducing this storytime. Use a short piece of a cardboard tube and pink felt. Cut a circle a little larger in diameter than the tube to cover one end. Snip around the edge, as shown. Use hot glue to attach the felt circle, covering one end of the tube. Cover the entire tube and the edges of the circle with a strip of felt the same width as the tube. Attach a length of elastic to the inside edges that will be on either side of your nose.

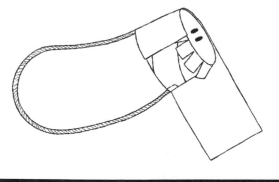

Activity: Toe Sock Puppet

Purchase a pair of toe socks and turn one into a puppet glove for your foot. Attach Velcro to the toes of the sock with hot glue, and use the pig puppets to recite the nursery rhyme "This Little Pig Went To Market" using your foot instead of

your hand! You may need to reduce the puppet pattern on the copier, so all five pigs will fit on your toes without overlapping too much.

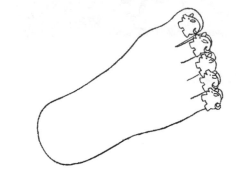

Take Home: Pig in a Puddle

Materials Needed

- Photocopies of pig
- Crayons
- Pink pipe cleaners
- Hole punch
- Cardboard tubes

Photocopy the pig pattern below and cut out one for each child. Punch out the holes for the pig's tail where indicated by the circle marked with the "X." Cut a length of cardboard tube approximately 1½ inch long to serve as a mud puddle for each pig. Cut two slits on opposite sides of the tube about ½ inch down. The pig will slide into these slits, allowing it to stand. After the children have colored their pig, let them attach a pipe cleaner tail that has been curled around a pencil to form a spiral. When that's done, the pig will be ready to sit in its "puddle."

Racecars

Start Your Engines!

Fingerplay: 5 Speedy Racecars

5 (4,3,2) speedy racecars
Around the track they zoom.
(Move hand in circular motion as if racing.)
One makes a pit stop, *(Remove one racecar.)*
While the others go VROOM!
*(Move hand in a circular motion as if going
around a racetrack and say "vroom" loudly!)*

<u>Closing Verse</u>
1 speedy racecar
Around the track it zooms.
It makes a pit stop, *(Remove last racecar.)*
Now none of them go VROOM!

Puppet & Palm Patterns

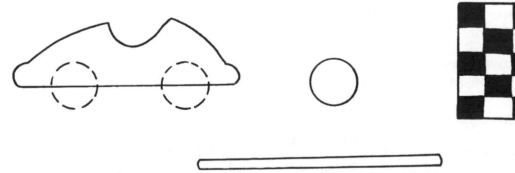

Hint: Assemble cars as shown using bright colors of felt. You can make these as flashy as you like by adding racing stripes, numbers, etc., with a fine-tipped permanent marker. Make the flag by cutting tiny squares of black felt and gluing them onto a larger white square in a checkered board pattern or drawing them on with a black marker.

Suggested Books to Share

Gackenbach, Dick. *Binky Gets a Car.* Clarion, 1983. When Binky gets his new car, he races around the neighborhood forgetting he must watch where he is going!

Jennings, Dana Andrew. *Me, Dad, & Number 6.* Harcourt Brace, 1997. A young boy helps his father and his friends rebuild an old car in hopes of driving it in the races.

Rex, Michael. *My Race Car.* Henry Holt and Co., 2000. A little boy, playing with his toy cars, imagines he is a real racecar driver.

Rockwell, Anne. *Cars.* Puffin Unicorn, 1984. Simple text and illustrations about all kinds of cars.

Todd, Mark. *Start Your Engines: A Countdown Book.* Callaway, 2000. A counting book with a racing theme and bright, colorful illustrations.

Props: Racecars and Racetracks

Bring in an assortment of small cars to discuss with the children. If you have a toy racetrack available, you can set it up as a display or hold miniature races before reading the stories.

Activity: Movement Song

Have the children form a circle and lead them in the following activity. Suit actions to the underlined word as you move around in the circle. If the group is young, make a masking tape "racetrack" on the floor for them to follow.

We'll Be Going Around the Racetrack

(To the tune "She'll be Coming Around the Mountain")

We'll be <u>hopping</u> around the racetrack when we go
We'll be <u>hopping</u> around the racetrack when we go
We'll be <u>hopping</u> around the racetrack
We'll be <u>hopping</u> around the racetrack
We'll be <u>hopping</u> around the racetrack when we go.

Substitute underlined words with other action words such as: skipping, walking, tiptoeing, jogging, crawling, etc.

Take Home: Racecars

Materials Needed

- Photocopies of racecar and wheels
- Crayons
- Paper brads

Prior to storytime, cut out a car and two wheels for each child from the patterns below. Using a hole puncher, punch a hole in the center of each wheel and on the car where indicated. Have children color the pieces. Demonstrate how to assemble. Depending on their age, children may need assistance with the paper brads.

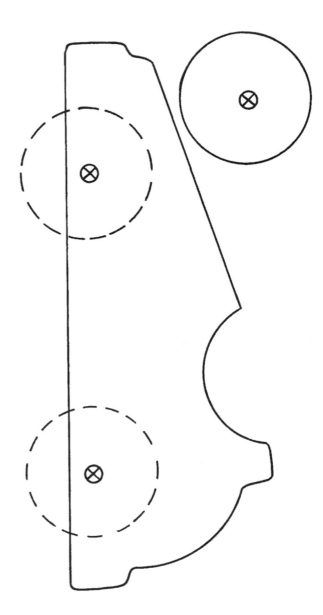

Snakes

Slither, Slither, Hiss, Hiss

Fingerplay: 5 Lazy Snakes

Down beside the lake,
Over near the dock,
1 (2,3,4) lazy snake(s)
Is (are) sunning on a rock.
Slither, slither, run! *(Say with excitement.)*
Here comes another one!
(Add one snake by "slithering" it to your glove.)

Closing Verse

Down beside the lake,
Over near the dock,
5 lazy snakes
Are sunning on a rock.
Now I'd better run
Before another one comes!

Puppet Pattern

Hint: These are so easy! Use any color felt you wish and as many colors as you wish. Apply faces with a permanent maker and glue Velcro to the back.

Suggested Books to Share

Buckley, Richard. *The Greedy Python.* Simon & Schuster, 1998. A greedy python eats everything he sees before finally eating himself.

Cannon, Janell. *Verdi.* Harcourt Brace, 1997. Verdi doesn't want to be like the older, lazier snakes he knows.

Noble, Trinka Hakes. *The Day Jimmy's Boa Ate the Wash.* Puffin Pied Piper, 1984. Jimmy brings his pet boa along on a field trip to a farm.

Ungerer, Tomi. *Crictor.* HarperCollins, 1958. A lady receives a large snake as a gift that becomes the town hero.

Walsh, Ellen Stoll. *Mouse Count.* Harcourt, Brace, Jovanovich, 1991. Ten little mice outsmart a hungry and greedy snake (a counting book).

Props: Snake Puppet

If you don't have a snake puppet, make one with an old sock or fashion a long tube from felt or cloth. These have been around forever, are still one of the cutest puppets you can make, and will be a great mascot for this storytime.

Activity: Follow the Leader

Make a masking tape "snake" outline throughout the room. Play "follow the leader" as you hiss and slither on the snaky trail. Make sure the snake's tail ends up curving back around to meet his head, so the fun can continue smoothly.

Take Home: Paper Plate and Hinged Snakes

Materials Needed for Paper Plate Snakes

- Six-inch paper plates
- Crayons
- Precut snake tongues
- Glue sticks

Cut snake tongues from red construction paper. Give each child a paper plate to color.

When they have finished, cut their plate in a spiral fashion, forming a head shape in the center. Try not to cut too many spirals so the snake will not be so "delicate." A pattern is included on pg. 41 in which the dotted line is a suggested cut line. Have children glue on the snakes' tongues after you have finished cutting the spiral.

Materials Needed for Hinged Snake

- Paper brads (at least three per child)
- Tagboard
- Crayons
- Hole punch

This snake can be as long as you would like! Prior to storytime, cut a head and tail and as many center pieces as you decide for each child from the patterns provided on pg. 41. Have children color all pieces and connect them together with the paper brads.

Pattern for Paper Plate Snake

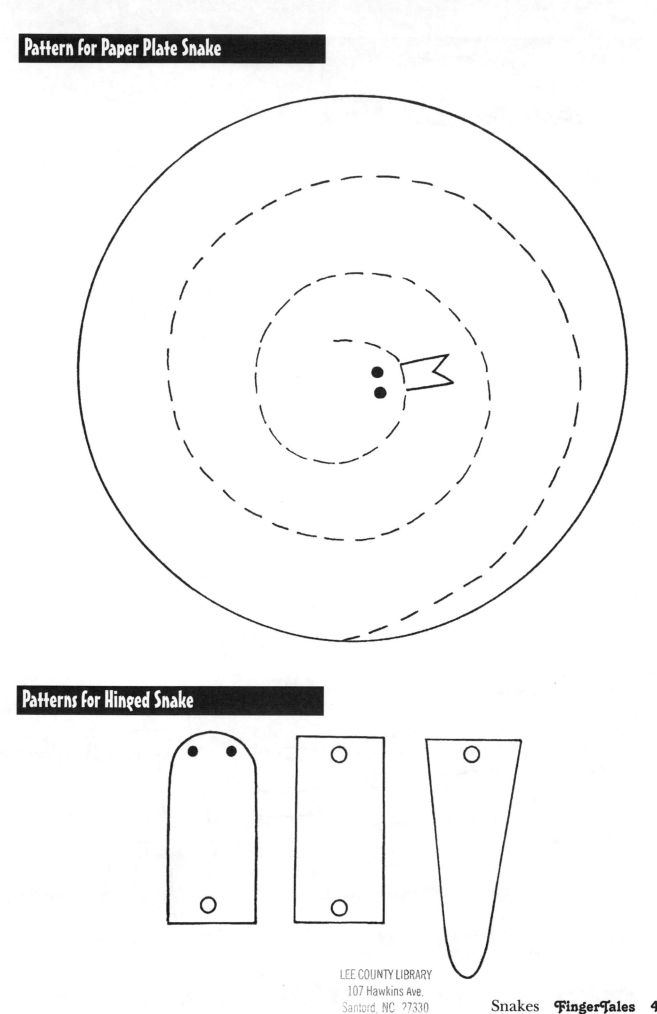

Patterns for Hinged Snake

Sneezes

Achoo!

Fingerplay: 5 Hungry Ants

5 (4,3,2) hungry ants
Marching in a line.
Came upon a picnic
Where they could dine.
They marched into the salad,
(Bounce hand in rhythm as if marching.)
They marched into the cake,
They marched into the pepper,
Uh oh! That was a mistake!
Achoo! *(Remove one ant as you "sneeze.")*

Closing Verse
1 hungry ant
Marching in a line.
Came upon a picnic
Where he could dine.
He marched into the salad,
He marched into the cake,
He marched into the pepper,
Uh oh! That was a mistake!
Achoo! *(Remove the last ant.)*

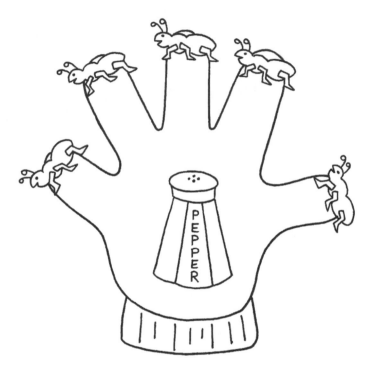

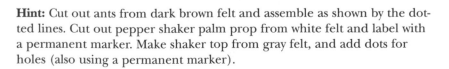

Puppet & Palm Patterns

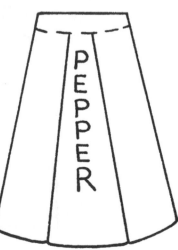

Hint: Cut out ants from dark brown felt and assemble as shown by the dotted lines. Cut out pepper shaker palm prop from white felt and label with a permanent marker. Make shaker top from gray felt, and add dots for holes (also using a permanent marker).

Suggested Books to Share

Brown, Ruth. *The Big Sneeze.* Lothrop, Lee & Shepard Books, 1985. A sleeping farmer sneezes when a fly lands on his nose and starts a chain reaction of events that effects the whole barnyard.

Edwards, Pamela D. *Slop Goes the Soup: A Noisy Warthog Word Book.* Hyperion, 2001. When a warthog sneezes while carrying soup to the table, he begins an onomatopoeic chain reaction that involves the whole family.

Gowler Greene, Rhonda. *Barnyard Song.* Atheneum, 1997. It starts when a bee sneezes, and suddenly all the animals in the barnyard catch the flu and lose their usual voices.

Shaw, Nancy. *Sheep Out to Eat.* Houghton Mifflin, 1992. The adorable sheep are all dressed up and dining out only to encounter pepper that brings on a sneeze that causes such a chain of disasters that they are asked to leave the restaurant!

Thomas, Patty. *"Stand Back," Said the Elephant, "I'm Going to Sneeze!"* William Morrow, 1990. When the elephant warns the animals that he's going to sneeze, they panic, remembering the damage his last sneeze caused. "The monkeys were sneezed right out of the trees, the parrot lost his feathers, the bees their stings" and so on.

Props: Tissues

Keep a box of tissues handy during this story-time! Odds are someone will be in need of one, sincerely or otherwise, especially after all the talk of sneezing.

Activity: Flannel Board

Using the patterns provided on pg. 44, make flowers for your flannel board from felt. Use bright colors and make as many as suitable for the age group of the children. Vary the length of the stems. Arrange the flowers as shown in the illustration. You may want to discuss "nose tickles" that make you sneeze, then proceed with the following rhyme.

5 Pretty Flowers

5 (4,3,2,1) pretty flowers
In the meadow grew.
"Hmmm," I said
"I bet they smell pretty too!"
I bent down to sniff,
But they tickled my nose!
Ah-choo! Oh, no!
(Playfully and with exaggeration!)
Away 1 flower blows! *(Remove one flower.)*

Take Home: Sneezing Elephant

Materials Needed

- Photocopies of elephant
- Crayons
- Tape
- Tissues

Prior to storytime, make photocopies of the elephant on pg. 45 and cut out one for each child. Also cut along the dotted line around the elephant's trunk. Have children color an elephant, then assist them in placing a tissue under its trunk and secure it in place with tape.

Flannel Board Patterns

Enlarge or shrink patterns to desired size.

sample flannel board

Sports

Play Ball!

Fingerplay: 5 Little Footballs

5 (4,3,2) little footballs
Trying hard a point to score.
1 makes a touchdown.
(Remove one football.)
Hear the crowd roar!
(Cheer!)

<u>Closing Verse</u>
1 little football
Trying hard a point to score.
It makes a touchdown.
(Remove last football.)
Hear the crowd roar!
(Cheer!)

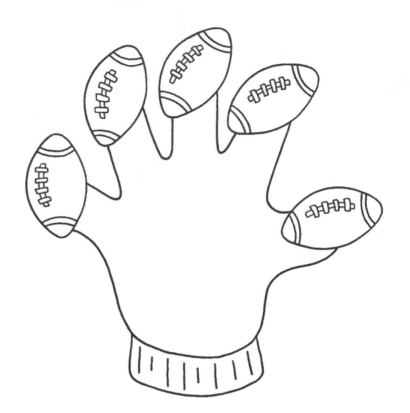

Puppet Pattern

Hint: Use brown felt for the footballs. The lacing on the football can be painted on with white fabric paint or cut from white felt.

Suggested Books to Share

Barber, Barbara E. *Allie's Basketball Dream.* Lee & Low, 1996. A young girl receives a basketball as a gift from her father, which she takes to the park in hopes of playing a game.

Bridwell, Norman. *Clifford's Sports Day.* Scholastic, 1996. Clifford goes to school with Emily Elizabeth and participates in the Sports Day activities—and ends up being a hero, too.

London, London. *Froggy Plays Soccer.* Viking, 1999. Froggy makes a mistake on the soccer field during the championship game.

Paxton, Tom. *The Jungle Baseball Game.* Morrow Jr. Books, 1999. All the jungle animals gather to play and watch a baseball game.

Yolen, Jane. *Moon Ball.* Simon & Schuster, 1999. Danny dreams he's playing baseball with the moon and the stars.

Props: Sports Equipment

Bring in a collection of sports equipment for the children to examine and discuss. You're sure to hear lots of stories!

Activity: Beanbag Toss

Make several beanbags to resemble assorted balls using the patterns on pg. 48 (orange circles for basketballs, white circles for baseballs, etc.) Add details, such as stitching on the baseball, with permanent markers. Set up containers for tossing or sit in a circle for a game of "hot potato" or catch. Make the beanbags from felt. Hot glue them around the edges leaving an area open until you fill them with any dry beans you have available. Finish gluing them closed and play ball! Make beanbags large enough so they are easy to grasp for little hands.

Take Home: Lace-up Footballs

Materials Needed

- Brown construction paper
- Scrap newsprint
- Yarn
- Masking tape

Prior to storytime, enlarge the football pattern on pg. 48 and photocopy and cut out two footballs for each child. Place the two footballs together and using a hole puncher, punch holes around the entire edge of the football. Measure a length of yarn long enough to sew the two balls together. Tie the end of the yarn through one set of holes securing the two balls together. Wrap masking tape around the other end of the yarn to form a needle for lacing, like the end of a shoestring. Have children lace the two footballs together. This may take some time and require some assistance from adults. When the children have almost completed their lacing, give them some newsprint scraps to stuff the balls with. After the lacing is complete, tie off the end and snip off the remaining yarn.

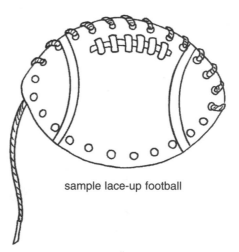

sample lace-up football

Beanbag Patterns

Enlarge patterns to desired size.

Football pattern also used for take home project.

Stars

Wish Upon a Star

Fingerplay: 5 Little Stars

In the night sky,
Dark as can be,
5 (4,3,2) little stars
Shone down on me.
The sun started rising, *(Raise sun.)*
Turning night into day.
And one little star
Twinkled away! *(Remove one star.)*

Closing Verse
In the night sky,
Dark as can be,
1 little star
Shone down on me.
The sun started rising, *(Raise sun.)*
Turning night into day.
And the last little star
Twinkled away! *(Remove last star.)*

Puppet & Palm Patterns

Hint: This fingerplay uses two puppets. Complete the star puppets and moon palm prop. Then, make the sun by cutting two circles from felt and gluing them together (leaving the bottom open for your finger). Glue the sunrays around the back circle. The glasses can be drawn on using paint or markers.

Suggested Books to Share

Carle, Eric. **Draw Me a Star.** G.P. Putman's Sons, 1992. Beginning with a star, an artist draws the universe!

Johnson, Crockett. **Harold's Trip to the Sky.** HarperCollins, 1957. Harold draws a rocket to the moon but ends up riding a shooting star home.

Schnur, Steven. **Night Lights.** Farrar, Straus & Giroux, 2000. A child counts the lights she sees, including the stars, before going to bed.

Stone, Kazuko G. **Goodnight Twinklegator.** Scholastic, 1990. Aligay plays connect the dots with the stars and ends up making a new friend named Twinklegator.

Trapani, Iza. **Twinkle, Twinkle, Little Star.** Whispering Coyote Press, 1994. A little girl goes on a journey through the sky with a star.

Props: Twinkling Stars

Drape a string of small, blinking, holiday lights from the ceiling over your storytime area. Dim the lights if possible, and ask the children to imagine that they are outside on a starlit night. Invite the children to do a little stargazing by lying on their backs while you read.

Activity: Movement Chant

Place several self-sticking, foil stars on the children's fingertips. Demonstrate how wiggling their fingers will make the stars look like they are twinkling. Then proceed by singing the song provided.

Twinkling Stars

(To the tune of "Twinkle, Twinkle, Little Star")
Twinkle, twinkle, little stars *(Wiggle fingers.)*
Stand and twinkle where you are.
(Stand up while wiggling fingers.)
Twinkle high and twinkle low,
(Put hands in the air then at your feet.)
Twinkle fast and twinkle slow.
(Shake hands fast then slow.)
Twinkle, twinkle, little stars,
(Continue wiggling fingers.)
Now sit and twinkle where you are.
(Sit back down.)

Take Home: Star Gazers or Star Pictures

Materials Needed for Star Gazers

- Toilet paper tubes
- Black construction paper
- Rubber bands
- Star stickers

Prior to storytime, cut circles from black paper large enough to cover the end of the paper tubes and be secured with a rubber band. Let children decorate a tube with star stickers. Assist them with covering one end of the tube with the paper circle and secure it with a rubber band. **This next part is to be done by you or an adult helper only:** Take a straight pin or a safety pin and make several small holes in the black paper on the end of the tube. When you look through the tube toward light, the holes will look like stars in the night sky!

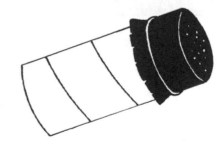

Materials Needed for Star Pictures

- Black construction paper
- Self-sticking stars
- Chalk

Give each child a piece of black paper and a sheet of stars. Have chalk available for them to use and encourage them to create pictures of the night sky.

Taxicabs

All Around the Town

Fingerplay: 5 Yellow Taxicabs

5 (4,3,2) yellow taxicabs
Delivering their fares.
Picking up and dropping off
People here and there.
They saw a filling station,
But they sped on past.
So one yellow taxicab
Ran out of gas! *(Remove one taxi.)*

<u>Closing Verse</u>
1 yellow taxicab
Delivering its fares.
Picking up and dropping off
People here and there.
It saw a filling station,
But it sped on past.
So the last yellow taxicab
Ran out of gas! *(Remove last taxi.)*

Puppet & Palm Patterns

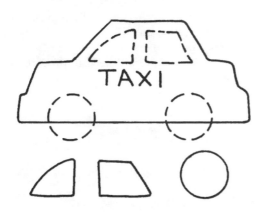

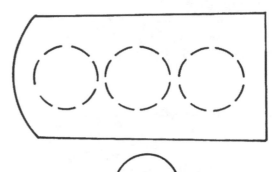

Hint: Assemble each taxi as shown. Print "TAXI" on the side of each with a fine-tipped permanent marker. Make the palm prop traffic light from black felt with a red, yellow and green light.

Suggested Books to Share

Barracca, Debra and Sal Barracca. *Adventures of Taxi Dog.* Dial, 1990. A taxi driver adopts a stray dog and they share the adventures of driving a taxi in New York.

Grover, Max. *Max's Wacky Taxi Day.* Harcourt Brace, 1997. Max spends the day as a taxi driver delivering passengers all over the city.

Maestro, Betsy and Giulio Maestro. *Taxi: A Book of City Words.* Clarion Books, 1989. A bright yellow taxi travels throughout a large city highlighting all the interests found there.

Porte, Barbara Ann. *Taxicab Tales.* Greenwillow Books, 1992. A collection of stories told to a family from their father who drives a taxicab.

Young, Ruth. *Daisy's Taxi.* Orchard Books, 1991. Daisy spends her days driving a different sort of taxi, a water taxi!

Props: Taxicab Story Chair

Make a cardboard taxi from a large box painted yellow that would fit over a small chair you could sit in while reading to the children. Remember that children have great imaginations, so it doesn't have to be very complicated for them to appreciate it.

Activity: Taxi Chat

Ask the children where they would like to go if they were riders in a taxi and what they would do when they got there. After they respond, proceed with the following song substituting the underlined word with their responses.

The Rider in the Taxi

(To the tune of "The Wheels on the Bus")

The rider in the taxi says,
"Take me to the park. Take me to the park. Take me to the park."
The rider in the taxi says,
"Take me to the park. I want to swing on the swings!"

If the children are young, you might want to suggest an activity and ask them where the taxi should take them, such as follows:

"If you wanted to check out a book where would you ask the taxi to take you?"

When the children respond "library" proceed with the song. Continue with other verses as long the children's interest holds and time allows.

Take Home: Car Tracks

Materials Needed

- Washable ink pads
- White or light colored paper
- Miniature cars

Collect and/or borrow as many miniature metal cars as possible. (If children are required to pre-register for your storytime, request each child bring an old one.) Provide each child with a car, an inkpad and a sheet of paper, and demonstrate how rolling the car wheels on the inkpad will let you make car tracks as you "drive" the car on the sheet of paper.

Hint: The cars will need to be rinsed off, as even "washable" ink can still be messy! If you're not afraid of making a mess and the cars are yours, regular inkpads can be used, but you will need to protect the children's clothing as well as the surrounding area.

Tools

My Toolbox

Fingerplay: 5 Little Nails

5 (4,3,2,1) little nails
Standing straight and steady.
Here comes the carpenter
With a hammer ready!
Bam! Bam! Bam! *(Remove one nail.)*

Puppet & Palm Patterns

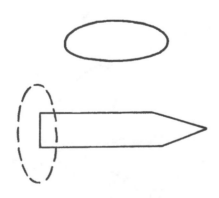

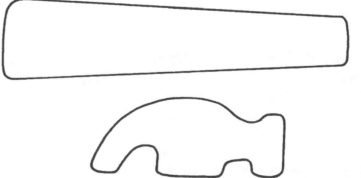

Hint: Use gray felt for the nails. For the palm prop, use gray
felt for the hammer's head and any color for the handle.

Suggested Books to Share

Lindbergh, Reeve. *If I'd Known Then What I Know Now.* Viking Penguin, 1996. A child grows older as the father works on endless projects in an attempt to finish their home.

Rockwell, Anne and Harlow Rockwell. *The Toolbox.* Aladdin Books, 1971. A young boy gives a simple description of the contents of his father's toolbox.

Shone, Venice. *Tools.* Cartwheel Books, 1990. Beautiful clear illustrations of every tool imaginable. Great book for introducing a storytime on the topic of tools.

Steig, William. *Solomon: The Rusty Nail.* Farrar, Straus & Giroux, 1985. Solomon discovers he is able to turn himself into a nail at will and uses this to escape from danger.

Tryon, Leslie. *Albert's Alphabet.* Atheneum, 1991. Albert, the goose, is the school carpenter who has been asked to build an alphabet for the school's walking path. He does this, using every tool imaginable.

Props: Tote Along Some Tools

Wear a nail apron and bring in a small toolbox filled with an assortment of small or plastic tools for discussion.

Activity: Action Rhyme

Lead children in the action rhyme "Johnny Works with One Hammer." Any name can be used. If you are working with a small group you could use the names of the children.

Johnny Works with One Hammer

1st verse
Johnny works with one hammer
(Move one fist up and down as if using a hammer.)
One hammer, one hammer, hammer.
Johnny works with one hammer,
Then he/she works with two.

2nd verse
Johnny works with two hammers, *(Two fists.)*

3rd verse
Johnny works with three hammers
(Two fists and bounce one knee.)

4th verse
Johnny works with four hammers,
(Two fists and two knees.)

Closing verse
Johnny works with five hammers
(Two fists, two knees and nod head.)
Five hammers, five hammers.
Johnny works with five hammers
Now his/her work is done!

Take Home: Craft Stick Hammers

Materials Needed

- Photocopies of hammer top
- Large wooden craft sticks
- Crayons
- Glue sticks

Copy and cut one hammer top for each child using the pattern below. Have children color both the hammer and the craft stick. Assist children if needed with gluing the stick to the uncolored side of the hammer. Fold on dotted line and finish gluing the hammer top together.

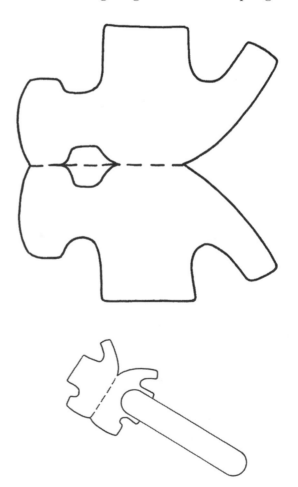

Wind

Whoosh!

Fingerplay: 5 Colorful Kites

Way up high
In the sky so blue,
5 (4,3,2,1) little kites
Flew and flew.
The wind blew hard,
The wind blew loud,
The wind blew the little red (yellow, blue,
orange, green) kite
Off to the clouds!
(Remove the appropriately colored kite.)

Puppet Patterns

Hint: Cut out kites from five different colors of
felt. Make the tails by tying felt shapes to dental
floss or sturdy thread and hot gluing to the back
of each kite. Hot glue Velcro to each kite.

Suggested Books to Share

Ets, Marie Hall. *Gilberto and the Wind.* Viking Press, 1963. A little boy tells about all the fun that he has playing with the wind.

Hutchins, Pat. *The Wind Blew.* Macmillan, 1974. This rhyming book tells about all the items the wind grabs from people before it finally blows out to sea.

Lobel, Arnold. *The Turnaround Wind.* Harper & Row, 1988. The wind blows very hard through this story, and if you turn the book upside-down the illustrations show yet another scene caused by the wind's mishaps.

McPhail, David. *The Day the Dog Said, "Cock-a-Doodle Doo!"* Scholastic, 1996. When the wind blows through the barnyard, the animals' sounds get all mixed up!

Weeks, Sarah. *Mrs. McNosh Hangs Up Her Wash.* Harper Festival, 1998. Mrs. McNosh spends the whole day washing everything from her clothes to the turkey she's roasting for dinner, and hanging them out to dry on her clothesline. Also a rhyming text.

Widman, Christine. *Housekeeper of the Wind.* Harper & Row, 1990. Yula, the wind's housekeeper, and the wind have disagreements and then make their apologies with gifts for each other.

Props: Construction Paper Kites

Make kites from brightly colored construction paper to hang from the ceiling. Use assorted colors of tissue paper for the tails, much like the suggested craft, only larger.

Activity: Match Game or Flannel Board

Clothesline Match Game

Using the patterns on pgs. 57 and 58, cut miniature clothes shapes from construction paper (or scrap material if available) in matching sets of two. Hang a clothesline across the room using sturdy cording or string. Give each child a clothespin and one item of clothing, but keep one complete set. Place the complete set in a laundry basket near you.

Pull out one item at a time and recite the following rhyme. Let the child with the matching item come up and hang it on the clothesline.

Washing Day

When washday comes along
I do my best to try
And wash my favorite (blue shirt, red dress, green pants, etc.),
Then hang it out to dry!

Hint: Over the years children have become less and less familiar with the concept of hanging clothes out to dry, so don't be surprised if this experience is new to them. Be sure of one thing though: most children love to hang objects with clothespins!

Flannel Board

Use the pattern on pg. 57 for the shirt only and make five shirts, each a different color, to use on your flannel board. String kite string across the flannel board to resemble a clothesline and position the shirts as if they were hanging from it. Proceed with the following fingerplay.

5 Colorful Shirts

5 (4,3,2,1) colorful shirts
Blowing in the breeze.
Drying on the clothesline
Pretty as you please.

But the wind blew too hard,
And a clothespin popped.
And the red shirt blew away,
(Remove shirt and insert appropriate color name.)
Before the wind stopped!

Take Home: Kites

Materials Needed

- Tagboard
- String or yarn
- Crayons
- Tape
- Tissue paper squares of different colors

Prior to storytime, cut tagboard into kite shapes and make a kite tail for each child. Make tails by tying three or four tissue paper squares, evenly spaced, to a length of yarn. Have children color their kites then let them tape a tail to it. Next, tape a length of yarn to the center of the kite as shown on pg. 58. The kites will receive a lot of punishment as the children attempt to fly them. This is why it's a good idea to use tagboard!

Enlarge patterns to desired size. See next page for additional pattern.

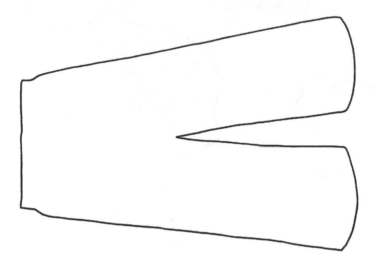

Illustration of Completed Take Home Kite

Finger Puppets

Ballerinas

Up on Our Toes!

Fingerplay: 5 Dancing Ballerinas

5 (4,3,2) dancing ballerinas
Prancing on their toes.
They twirl and spin and jump,
Then off the stage one goes!
(Remove one ballerina.)

<u>Closing Verse</u>
1 dancing ballerina
Prancing on her toes.
She twirls and spins and jumps
Then off the stage she goes!
(Remove the last ballerina.)

Puppet Patterns

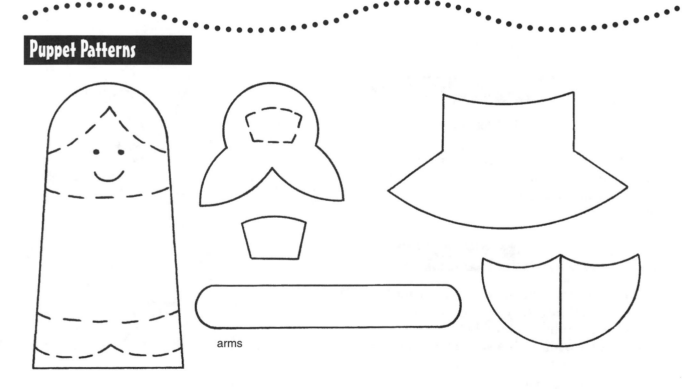

arms

Hint: Use a variety of skin color felts for these puppets. Cut two puppet bodies for the front and back. Completely assemble the front of each puppet, including drawing dotted lines as guides to place the clothes. Then glue on the back, leaving the bottom open for your finger. Next, glue the arm piece to the back. Finish by adding facial features with a fine-tipped permanent marker.

Suggested Books to Share

Allen, Debbie. *Dancing in the Wings.* Dial Books, 2000. Sassy has dreams of becoming a star ballerina and hopes that the visitor to her dance class believes she will be.

Auch, Mary Jane. *Hen Lake.* Holiday House, 1995. Poulette is a hen ballerina who challenges an obnoxious peacock to a talent show. She and the other hens will perform the ballet "Hen Lake."

Auch, Mary Jane. *Peeping Beauty.* Holiday House, 1993. More than anything else, Poulette wants to be a famous ballerina, so when a fox claiming to be a talent scout from New York City shows up, she has no choice but to perform in a ballet with him.

Carlson, Nancy. *Harriet's Recital.* Carolrhoda, 1982. Harriet is overwhelmed with stage fright at the thought of her recital but overcomes it in time for her debut.

Holabird, Katharine. *Angelina Ballerina.* Pleasant Company, 2000. Angelina loves to dance and wants to become a ballerina more than anything else in the world.

Sîs, Peter. *Ballerina!* Greenwillow, 2001. A little girl dresses in costumes of different colors as she imagines herself dancing on stage.

Props: Ballerina Doll or Puppet

If you have a ballerina doll or puppet, it would be the perfect prop for this storytime. If not, bring in old tutus, toe shoes, etc., that are available, or even a musical jewelry box that has a ballerina who twirls when the box is opened.

Activity: Dance Recital

Provide appropriate background music for ballet, and lead a freestyle dance recital. (It would be helpful if you have a little ballet experience. If not, there are lots of books available for beginners!) Also, lead the children in the movement activity below.

Ballerinas
(To the tune of "Are You Sleeping")

Ballerinas,
Ballerinas.
Twirl around,
Twirl around.
Dance up on your tiptoes,
Dance up on your tiptoes.
Now sit down,
Now sit down.

Take Home: Ballerina

Materials Needed

- Photocopies of ballerina
- Plastic straws (or unsharpened pencils)
- Crayons or markers
- Tape

Cut ballerinas from pattern on pg. 63 prior to storytime. Have children color their ballerina, then assist them with taping the straw to the inside as shown. Fold on the dotted line and then tape closed. To make the ballerina twirl, demonstrate to children how to place the straw between their palms and rub back and forth in opposite directions.

Howdy Partners!

Fingerplay: 5 Rowdy Cowboys

5 (4,3,2) rowdy cowboys
On a round-up out west.
Wearing ten-gallon hats,
Cowboy boots and vests.
The cattle started running
A stampede was on the way.
So 1 rowdy cowboy
Galloped away! *(Remove one cowboy.)*

<u>Closing Verse</u>
1 rowdy cowboy
On a round-up out west.
Wearing a ten-gallon hat,
Cowboy boots and vest.
The cattle started running
A stampede was on the way.
So the last rowdy cowboy
Galloped away! *(Remove last cowboy.)*

Puppet Patterns

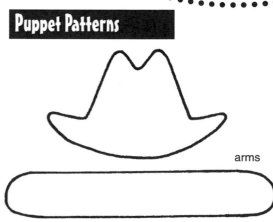

arms

Hint: Cut two puppet bodies out of a skin-tone color of felt. Finish the front completely using dotted lines as guides to place the clothes. The boots are attached rather low on the body (see illustration) making these puppets a little taller than the others. Next, glue the back and front together leaving the bottom open for your finger, and then the arm piece across the back. Finish by adding the facial features with a fine-tipped permanent marker.

Suggested Books to Share

Heap, Sue. *Cowboy Baby.* Candlewick Press, 1998. Cowboy Baby and his pals get ready to go to bed with some help from Sheriff Pa.

Hooker, Ruth. *Matthew the Cowboy.* Albert Whitman & Co., 1990. After receiving a cowboy suit for his birthday, Matthew takes an imaginary trip out west where he tames wild horses and captures rustlers.

Lowell, Susan. *The Three Little Javelinas.* Rising Moon, 1992; and *Little Red Cowboy Hat.* Henry Holt & Co., 1997. Southwestern versions of "The Three Little Pigs" and "Little Red Riding Hood."

Rounds, Glen. *Cowboys.* Holiday House, 1991. The story follows a cowboy from sunup to bedtime, as he rounds up cattle stampeding from a bolt of lightning to playing cards in the bunkhouse after supper.

Teague, Mark. *How I Spent My Summer Vacation.* Crown Publishers, 1995. A boy gives an oral report to his classmates describing his trip out west to visit his aunt and the unexpected adventures he encountered.

Props: Cactus

Using the pattern provided on pg. 67 as a guide, cut a large cactus from pieces of a cardboard box. Paint it green (spray paint works very well) and add tissue paper flowers as accents if you like. Cut slots on the pieces as indicated by the dotted lines. Slide the two pieces together so the bottom forms an "X." This will allow the cactus to stand, but it will help stabilize it if you secure the two pieces together with packing tape as indicated in the picture. The cactus will still fold flat for storing.

Next, make stones to circle a campfire with gray tissue paper. Crumple newspaper to form several stones about the size of a baseball. Wrap with masking tape and cover papier-mâché style with gray tissue and glue. Lay the stones in a circle on the floor and use red and yellow tissue paper as flames in the center. Add twigs you've collected to the center of the circle as shown. When finished, you and your little cowpokes can enjoy stories as you sit around the campfire!

Activity: Roundup

To give the children a chance to stretch their legs, have a "roundup" between stories. Enlarge and cut out the cow pattern below and hide copies in your storytime area. Near you, have a pen for the cattle. This could be a shoe box decorated to look like a corral or a fence borrowed from a play farm set, etc. To begin, ask the children to help you round up the cattle. As they find the cattle have them place them in the "corral." The roundup is over when you ring the dinner bell. (A triangle from your musical instruments would be great, but any bell would do.)

Take Home: Cowboy Hats

Materials Needed

- Enlarged photocopy of hat
- White construction paper
- Crayons
- Tape

Enlarge hat pattern below on copier to fit construction paper. Prior to storytime, cut out hats from construction paper. Also cut along the dotted line in the center of the hat. Have children color the hats then assist them in curving the brim up on one side and taping it to the spot marked with the "X." Then do the other side. Curling the brim up the side gives the hat that "ten-gallon" look.

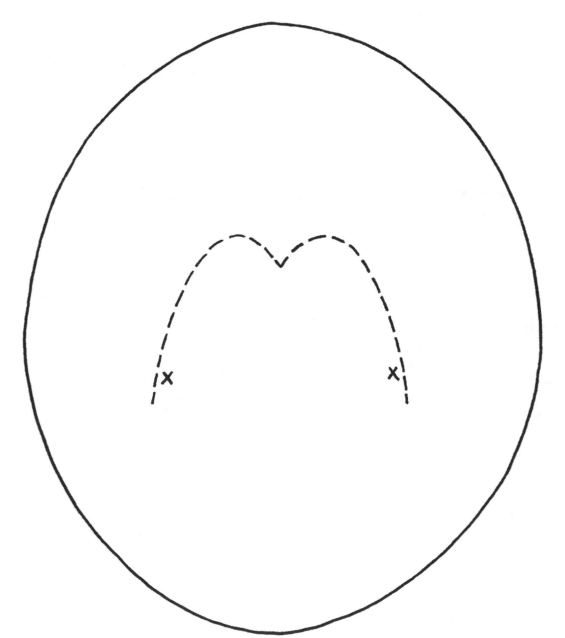

Cactus Prop Patterns

Enlarge patterns to desired size.

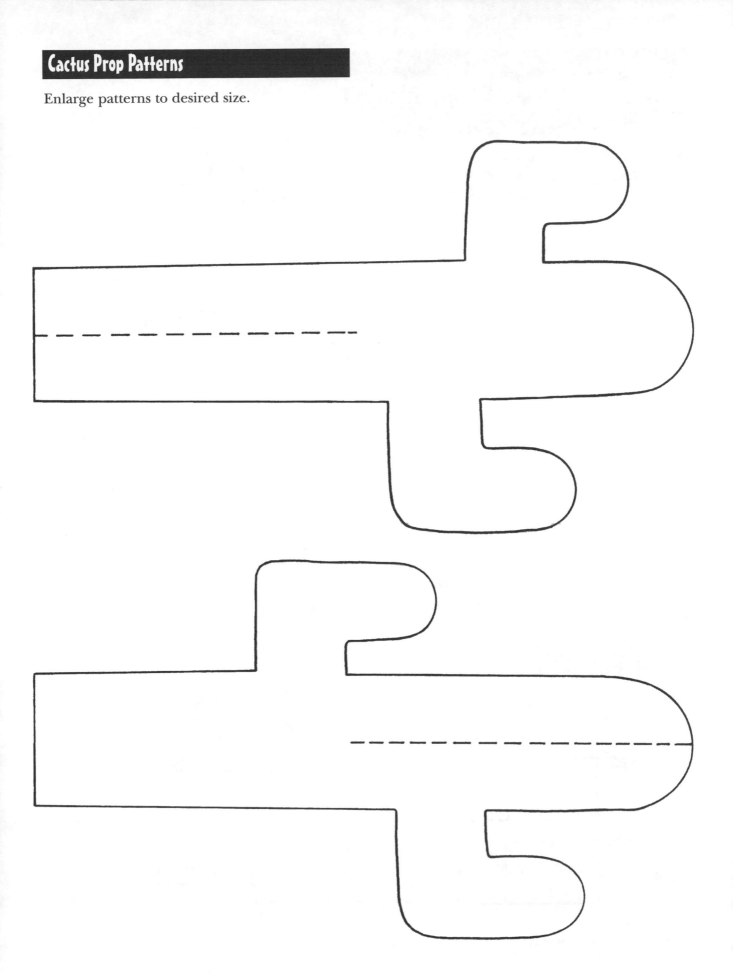

Houses

Home Is Where the Heart Is!

Fingerplay: 5 Little Houses

1 (2,3,4) little house (houses)
All alone it (they) stood.
Then another one was built
(Add one house.)
There grows the neighborhood!

<u>Closing Verse</u>
5 little houses
All together they stood.
On a beautiful street
In a happy neighborhood!

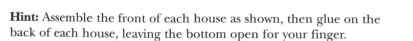

Puppet Patterns

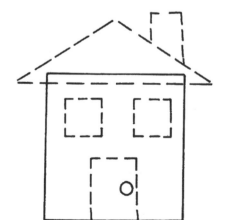

Hint: Assemble the front of each house as shown, then glue on the back of each house, leaving the bottom open for your finger.

Suggested Books to Share

Carle, Eric. *A House for a Hermit Crab.* Picture Book Studios, 1988. A hermit crab searches for a new home when he outgrows his old shell. When he finds a new one, he feels it is too plain and goes about decorating it using items he finds in the sea.

Dr. Seuss. *In a People House.* Random House, 1972. A mouse gives a bird a tour of a house and its contents while the occupants are not home.

Hoberman, Mary Ann. *A House Is a House for Me.* Viking, 1997. The book sums it up by stating "It seems that whatever you see is either a house or it lives in a house."

Wood, Audrey. *The Napping House.* Harcourt, 1985. The occupants of this house are happily sleeping until a biting flea starts a chain reaction.

Ziefert, Harriet. *The Cow in the House.* Viking, 1997. A man who is annoyed by the noise in his house gets advice from a wise man.

Props: Houses Around the World

Collect pictures of different styles of houses from around the world made of assorted materials to show and discuss with the children. If the group consists of younger children, use the story "The Three Little Pigs" to discuss houses and different construction materials. You may even want to lead the children in a retelling of the story focusing on the homes the little pigs built with the houses cut from felt for your flannel board.

Activity: Flannel Board

Enlarge the patterns provided on pg. 70 so they will be very easy for the children to see on your flannel board. Cut the shapes from different colored felt to use with the activity below.

A House of Shapes
Some houses are wood,
And some are stone.
But let's build one
With shapes alone.

Start with a square,
(Place square on flannel board.)
But we won't stop.
Add a triangle
Up on the top. *(Place triangle for roof.)*
Then a rectangle
For the door. *(Place rectangle on square.)*
Now square windows
1, 2, 3, 4! *(Place four squares for windows.)*
A little circle
Just for fun. *(Place circle for doorknob.)*
Now our shape house
Is all done!

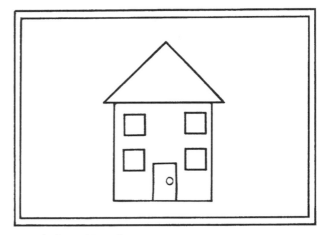

sample flannel board

Take Home: Peek-a-boo Houses

Materials Needed

- Photocopies of houses
- White paper
- Crayons
- Glue sticks

Photocopy one house on pg. 71 for each child on colored paper. Cut the dotted lines on the door and the windows and fold on the solid lines making the windows and the door into "flaps." Glue a white piece of paper (the same size as the one the house is printed on) to the back of the house. Now when the "flaps" are open, there will be white paper for the children to draw on. After storytime, let the children draw people and/or objects behind the "flaps" that they might see in their houses.

Enlarge patterns to desired size.

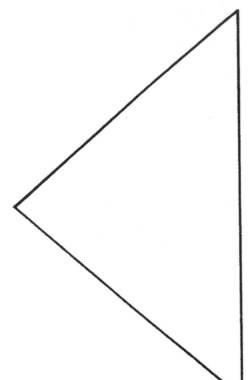

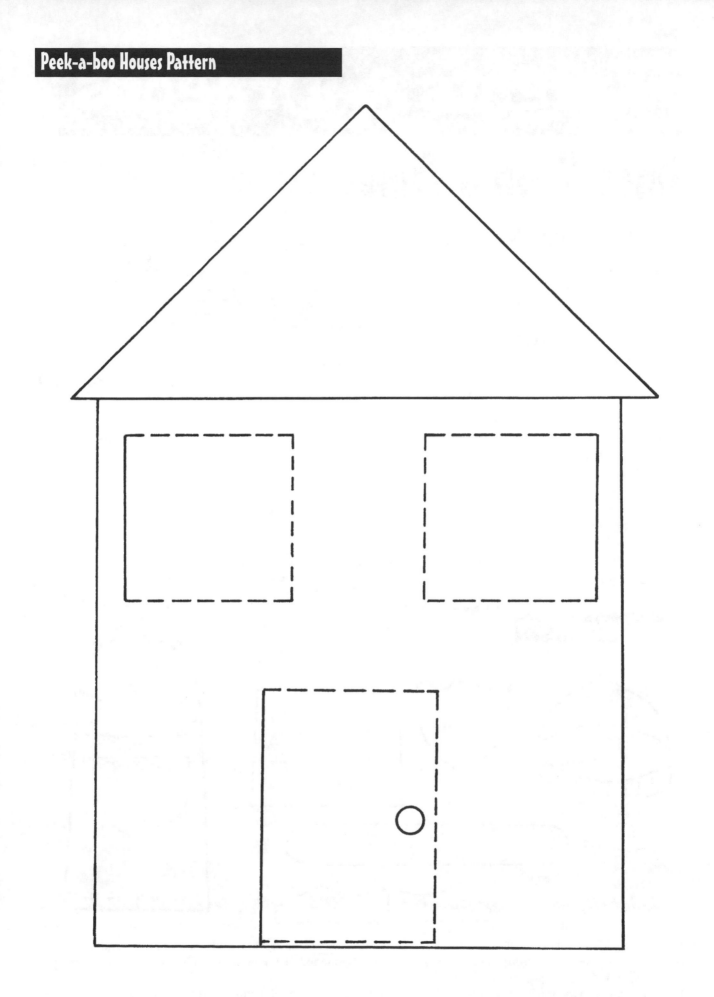

Knights & Dragons

Once Upon a Time

Fingerplay: 5 Knights in Shining Armor

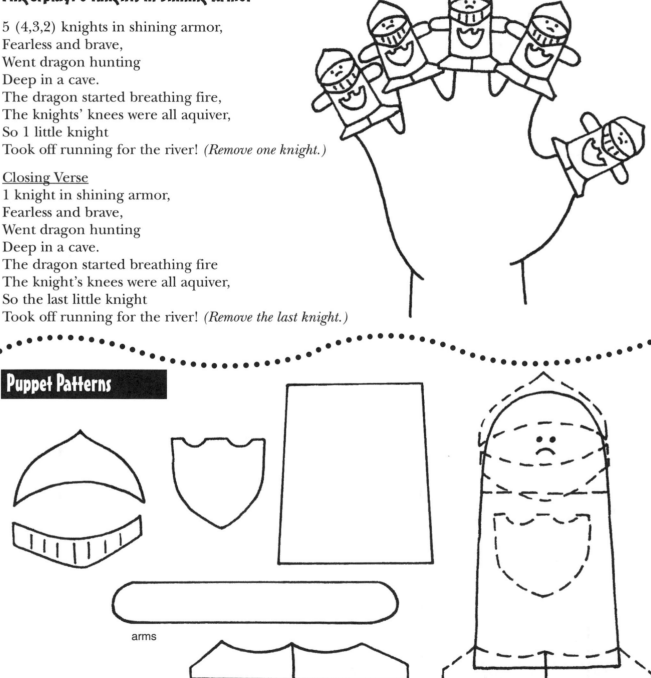

5 (4,3,2) knights in shining armor,
Fearless and brave,
Went dragon hunting
Deep in a cave.
The dragon started breathing fire,
The knights' knees were all aquiver,
So 1 little knight
Took off running for the river! *(Remove one knight.)*

<u>Closing Verse</u>
1 knight in shining armor,
Fearless and brave,
Went dragon hunting
Deep in a cave.
The dragon started breathing fire
The knight's knees were all aquiver,
So the last little knight
Took off running for the river! *(Remove the last knight.)*

Puppet Patterns

arms

Hint: Cut two puppet bodies and the arm piece out of a skin-tone color of felt. Cut the suit of armor and helmet from gray felt. Use five different colors of felt for the shields, one for each knight. Assemble the front of the puppet using the dotted lines as guides for placement of armor, then glue on the back body piece, leaving the bottom open for your finger. Then attach the arm piece. Finish by drawing on the facial features and the lines on the face guard.

Suggested Books to Share

Christelow, Eileen. *Henry and the Dragon.* Clarion, 1984. Henry the rabbit is convinced there is a dragon in his yard. He sets a trap for the dragon but only catches his dad who doesn't want to hear any more about the dragon!

Deedy, Carmen Agra. *The Library Dragon.* Peachtree, 1994. The new school librarian is a real dragon until a little girl wins her over and things start changing in the library. One by one the dragon's scales fall off to reveal the true librarian (see "Good-bye Game" below.)

De Paola, Tomie. *The Knight and the Dragon.* G.P. Putnam's Sons, 1980. A knight and a dragon study books in preparation for battling each other until a princess gives them new books to read that leads to a friendship and a business venture between them instead. (Makes a great flannel board story!)

Munsch, Robert N. *The Paper Bag Princess.* Annick Press, 1980. Princess Elizabeth sets out to rescue Prince Ronald from a dragon by outwitting him, only to find out that Ronald isn't much of a prince after all.

Props: Dragon or Knight Puppet

Use a dragon puppet to introduce this storytime. If you don't have one available, enlarge the knight finger puppet on the copier until it is large enough to fit your hand and make a hand puppet to use as the prop for this storytime.

Activity: Dragon Scale Hunt

You'll need to recruit help for this activity. While you are with the children in storytime, ask a co-worker to hide dragon scales, cut from green paper, in the children's books. (If possible, use glossy paper.) At the end of storytime, invite the children to the designated area to hunt for the scales that have fallen from the dragon in their library. If needed, give the children a limit on how many each may find (one for each hand works well).

Take Home: Castles and Shields

Materials Needed for Castles

- Photocopies of castle (preferably on tag-board or card stock)
- Crayons
- Tape

Make photocopies of castle pattern on pg. 74 and cut them out prior to storytime. Have children color castles, then assist them in folding them on the four dotted lines, forming the castle into a square shape. Slide the tab under the last section of the castle and secure with tape. Castles will stand on flat surfaces.

Materials Needed for Shields

- Cardboard
- Aluminum foil
- Glue sticks

Enlarge the shield provided on pg. 75 to any size, and use it as a pattern to cut shields from scrap cardboard for each child. I know this is tough work, but cardboard will work best! Hot glue an arched strip of cardboard to the back of each shield to act as a handle. These can be decorated in many ways. Because of their heavy weight they can be painted, colored with markers or decorated collage-style with paper or aluminum foil and glue sticks.

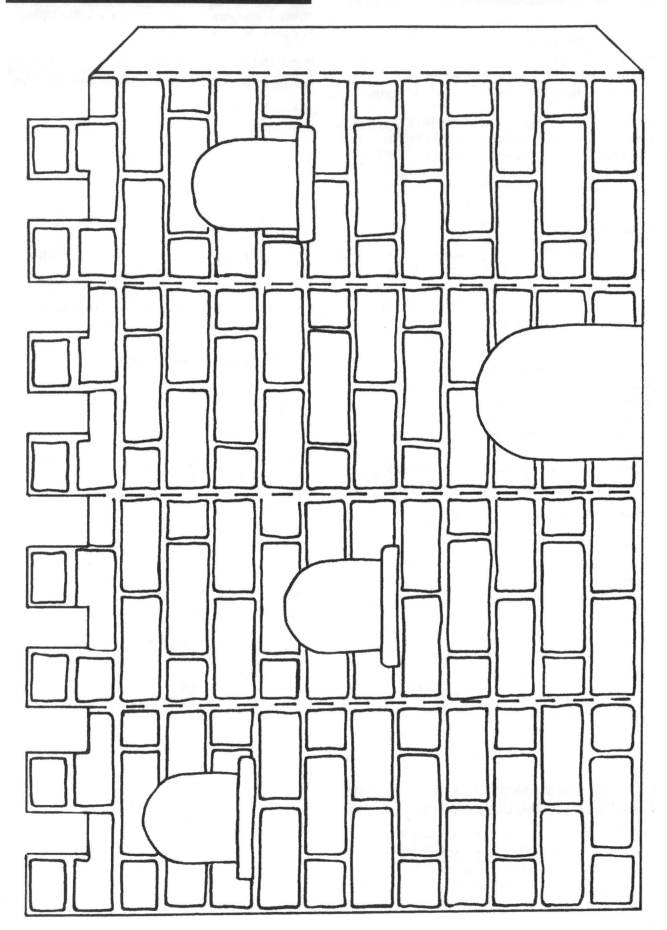

Shield Pattern

Enlarge pattern to desired size.

Magic

Abracadabra!

Fingerplay: 5 Magic Rabbits

5 (4,3,2) magic rabbits,
Each in a tall black hat.
Along comes a magician
Who gives each one a pat. *(Pat head.)*
Then he waves his magic wand
High above their ears.
Abracadabra, poof! *(Remove one rabbit.)*
1 rabbit disappears!

Closing Verse
1 magic rabbit,
He's in a tall black hat.
Along comes a magician
Who gives him a pat. *(Pat head.)*
Then he waves his magic wand
High above his ears.
Abracadabra, poof! *(Remove last rabbit.)*
The last rabbit disappears!

Puppet Patterns

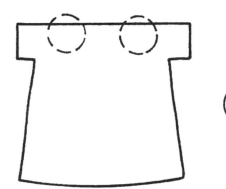

Hint: Cut two hats from black felt. Cut out parts for the rabbit and assemble it onto one of the two hats. When that is complete, glue the second hat to the back of the first one, "sandwiching" the rabbit's neck in between. Leave the bottom open for your finger.

Suggested Books to Share

De Paola, Tomie. *Strega Nona's Magic Lessons.* Harcourt Brace Jovanovich, 1982. Big Anthony wants to take magic lessons from Strega Nona.

Lester, Helen. *The Revenge of the Magic Chicken.* Houghton Mifflin, 1990. When the magic chicken attempts to use his pickle wand to play a trick on the wizard and the fairy, he has trouble remembering the magic chant.

Schubert, Ingrid and Dieter. *Abracadabra.* Front Street, 1997. A wizard is casting spells on the forest animals who must work together to stop him.

Simmons, Steven. *Alice and Greta: A Tale of Two Witches.* Crown Publishers, 1997. Two little witches are in school to learn magic, which they use in opposing ways.

Strete, Craig. *Little Coyote Runs Away.* G.P. Putnam's Sons, 1997. When little coyote runs away, his mother reminds him to take his special bag filled with magic items to protect him.

Props: Magic Pickle Wand or Rabbit Puppet

Magic Pickle Wand

Make a magic pickle wand to use while reading *The Revenge of the Magic Chicken.* While reading the book you can wave the wand while the children help you chant the magic spell:

Pickle, pickle, bright and green
Make me something very mean.

Directions: Using the pickle pattern on pg. 79, cut two from bright green felt. Hot glue around the edges leaving an opening for stuffing with fiberfill. After stuffing, insert a wooden dowel and finish gluing the pickle closed around the dowel. Use a fine-tipped permanent maker to add the squiggle lines on the pickle.

Rabbit Puppet

This is another finger puppet that can easily be adapted to use as a hand puppet. Simply enlarge the pattern on a copier until it is a suitable size for your hand, and assemble.

Activity: Flannel Board

Using the pattern provided on pg. 78, make rabbits in hats using white felt for the rabbits and six different colors of felt for the hats. You will also need a scarf. Place each hat on the flannel board, one at a time, as the children name each color. Ask them to try and remember each color. Then say the chant below.

First let's say a magic chant.
Now you see them, now you can't!
(Cover flannel board with scarf.)
Say abracadabra loud and clear.
(Pause for children to respond.)
Which one now has disappeared?
(Remove one with the scarf and keep it hidden until the children respond to the question.)

Continue playing, removing one color each time.

Take Home: Magic Wands

Make magic wands. If you read *The Revenge of the Magic Chicken,* you can make the pickle wands from the "props" section. If not, make star wands using the pattern on pg. 79.

Materials Needed

- Precut star shapes or pickles
- Pipe cleaners or straws
- Tape, glue sticks, glitter

Let each child tape a star or pickle to a pipe cleaner or straw. Use a glue stick to cover the star shape for the glitter. Allow children to sprinkle glitter on the shape while holding it over a paper plate to catch the excess glitter.

Flannel Board Pattern

Enlarge or shrink pattern to desired size.

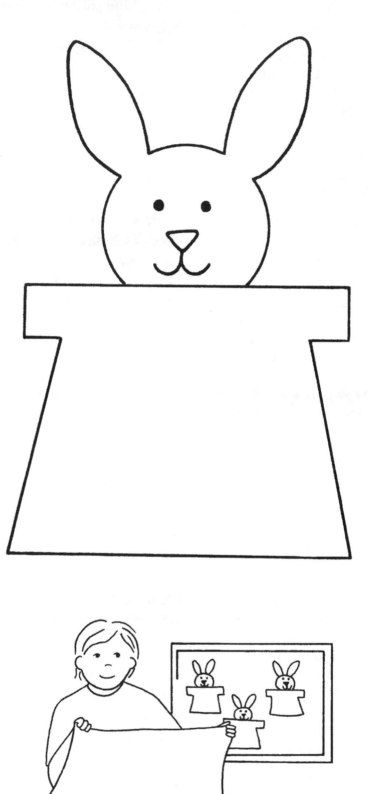

Magic Pickle and Star Wand Patterns

Enlarge patterns to desired size.

Penguins

Our Chilly Friends

Fingerplay: 5 Chilly Penguins

Slipping and sliding
To and fro,
5 (4,3,2) chilly penguins
Were playing in the snow.
They climbed up high *(Slowly raise hand.)*
To the top of a hill,
And one slid down —
(Remove one penguin and "slide" it down.)
Oh what a spill!

<u>Closing Verse</u>
Slipping and sliding
To and fro,
1 chilly penguin
Was playing in the snow.
He climbed up high *(Slowly raise hand.)*
To the top of a hill,
And he slid down —
(Remove last penguin and "slide" it down.)
Oh what a spill!

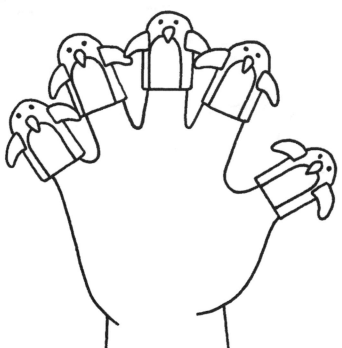

Puppet Patterns

Hint: Assemble the front of the puppet, as shown, using the dotted lines as guides. (Cut the eyes from white felt and draw the pupil with a black marker.) Glue the back onto the finished front, leaving the bottom opened for your finger.

Suggested Books to Share

Alborough, Jez. *Cuddly Dudley.* Candlewick, 1995. Dudley leaves home to escape from the constant hugs from his family only to miss the attention later.

Lester, Helen. *Tacky the Penguin.* Houghton Mifflin, 1988. Tacky becomes the hero after he tricks the hunters who are looking for penguins.

Pfister, Marcus. *Penguin Pete.* North-South Books, 1994. A story about a little penguin and his adventures.

Rigby, Rodney. *Hello, This Is Your Penguin Speaking.* Hyperion, 1992. Penguin wishes he could fly, and through trial and error succeeds in becoming first an airplane, then a space shuttle.

Seibold, J. Otto. *Penguin Dreams.* Chronicle Books, 1999. A little penguin dreams he can fly.

Props: Penguin Hat

Buy a black knit hat, or make one from felt, and turn it into a penguin hat for your story-time. Just add a white belly, yellow beak and eyes to the black hat, and you will be ready for some chilly stories!

Activity: Flannel Board

Make penguins out of felt from the patterns provided on pg. 82. Use five different colors for their hats. Cut five snowballs from white felt. Make them large enough to cover the penguin, but small enough to leave its hat visible when covered. Place the penguins on the flannel board, and proceed with the following rhyme.

5 Little Penguins
5 (4,3,2,1) little penguins standing in a row.
Rolling down the hill, comes a big ball of snow!
(Hold up first snowball.)
The snowball hits a bump and comes down with a splat. *(Cover first penguin.)*
Now all you can see is the little penguin's hat!

Continue until all penguins are covered. Then let the children call out the colors of each hat as you uncover the penguins.

Take Home: Egg Penguins and Bag Puppets

Materials Needed for Egg Penguins

- Plastic Easter eggs (one per child)
- Modeling clay
- Glue sticks
- White and orange felt scraps
- Permanent black marker

Prior to storytime, fill the wide end of the eggs with modeling clay (enough to make the eggs stand and wobble), and cut out bellies and beaks from felt. Let each child glue a belly and beak on an egg, and assist if necessary with dotting on eyes with the marker.

Materials Needed for Paper Bag Puppets

- Lunch-size paper bags
- Crayons
- Glue sticks
- Photocopies of puppet parts

Using the patterns on pg. 83, precut enough puppet parts so each child has a set. Give each child a paper bag and the puppet parts to color. When they have finished, assist them in gluing the parts to the bag.

Enlarge or shrink patterns to desired size.

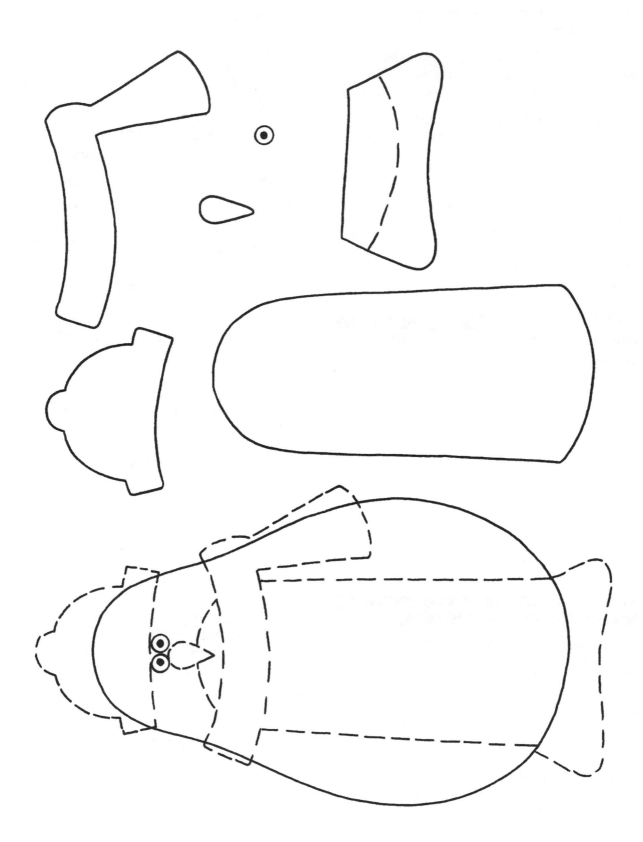

Enlarge patterns to fit lunch-size bag.

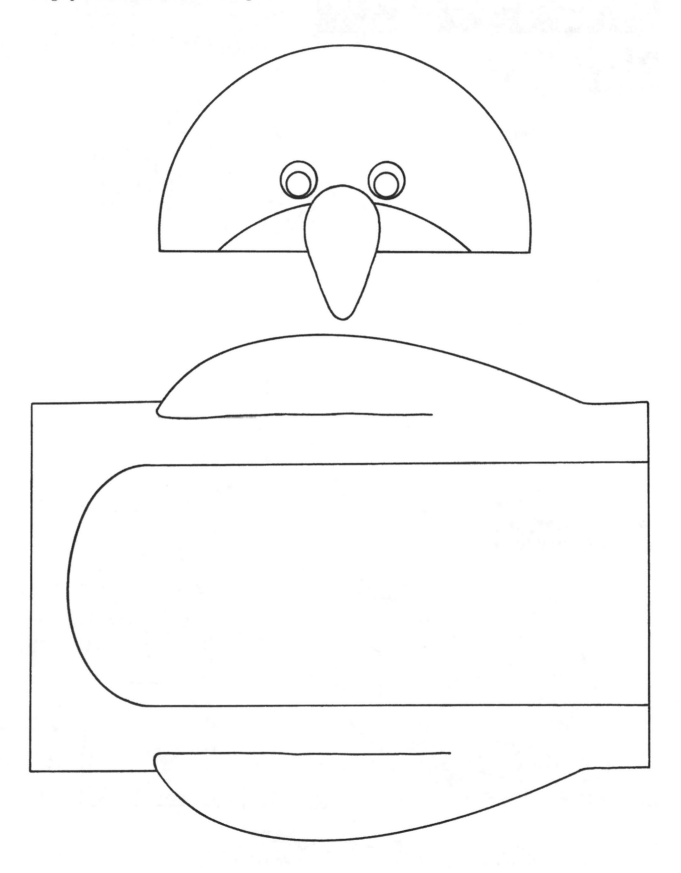

Rockets

Blast Off!

Fingerplay: 5 Fast Rockets

1 (2,3,4) fast rocket(s)
Blasting off to space.
Here comes another one. *(Add one rocket.)*
Now they can race!

<u>Closing Verse</u>
5 fast rockets
Let the race begin!
They'll circle the moon,
Then home they'll zoom.
Which do you think will win?

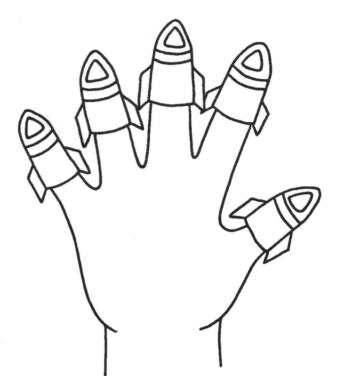

Puppet Patterns

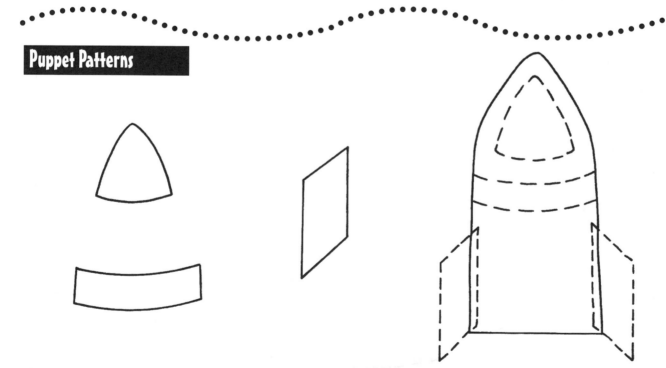

Hint: Cut two rocket shapes (one for the front and one for the back) and two fins from gray felt for each puppet. Cut the window for each rocket from white felt. Use a different color felt for the stripe for each rocket. (If the rockets can be distinguished by the color of their stripes, the children will be able to reply to the question of who will win by color.) Assemble the front as shown and then glue on the back, leaving the bottom open for your finger.

Suggested Books to Share

Asch, Frank. *Mooncake.* Aladdin, 1988. Bear is curious about how the moon tastes, so he builds a rocket and plans his trip, but it's getting close to hibernation time!

Delhomme, Jean-Philippe. *Visit to Another Planet.* Callaway, 2000. A family decides to visit another planet for their vacation instead of their usual trip to Connecticut.

Johnson, Crockett. *Harold's Trip to the Sky.* HarperCollins, 1957. Harold draws a rocket with his purple crayon and rockets to the moon!

Mitton, Tony. *Roaring Rockets.* Kingfisher, 1997. A book with a rhyming text about traveling through space in a rocket.

Yorinks, Arthur. *Tomatoes from Mars.* HarperCollins, 1999. A scientist works to save the planet from an invasion of huge tomatoes from Mars.

Props: Anything "Spacey"

There are many different props you can use to introduce this storytime, from scale models of rockets, solar systems and astronauts, to pictures of the same. If possible, hang planets and stars from the ceiling, using fishing line. These can be made from styrofoam balls or papier-mâché.

Activity: Flannel Board Poem

Cut out the flannel board figures, using the patterns provided on pg. 86. Use the appropriate color felt for the planets and stars. This presentation will be more appealing if your flannel board is black. When you are ready, recite the following poem.

Little Rocket's Trip
A little rocket *(Place rocket on board.)*
Roared off one day *(Move rocket upward.)*
On a trip into space,
So far away.
While zooming about,

He saw some stars *(Add several stars to board.)*
Then he circled around
The planet Mars. *(Add Mars.)*
He saw planet Saturn, *(Add Saturn.)*
And the man in the moon, *(Add the moon.)*
Then he saw planet Earth, *(Add Earth.)*
And back home he zoomed!
(Lower rocket to bottom of the board.)

Take Home: Rocket Kites

Materials Needed

- Photocopies of rocket (preferably on tagboard)
- Crayons
- Tape
- Yarn or string

Photocopy and cut both pieces of the rocket ahead of time for each child using the patterns on pg. 87. Cut the slit, indicated by the dotted line, on both pieces, and punch the hole in the larger piece. Have children color each piece of the rocket. Assist with assembling the pieces if needed, then secure with tape as shown. Tie a piece of yarn approximately two feet long to the rocket.

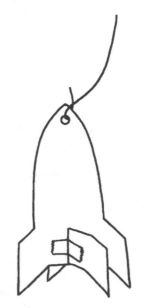

Enlarge patterns to desired size.

Rocket Kite Patterns

Enlarge patterns to desired size.

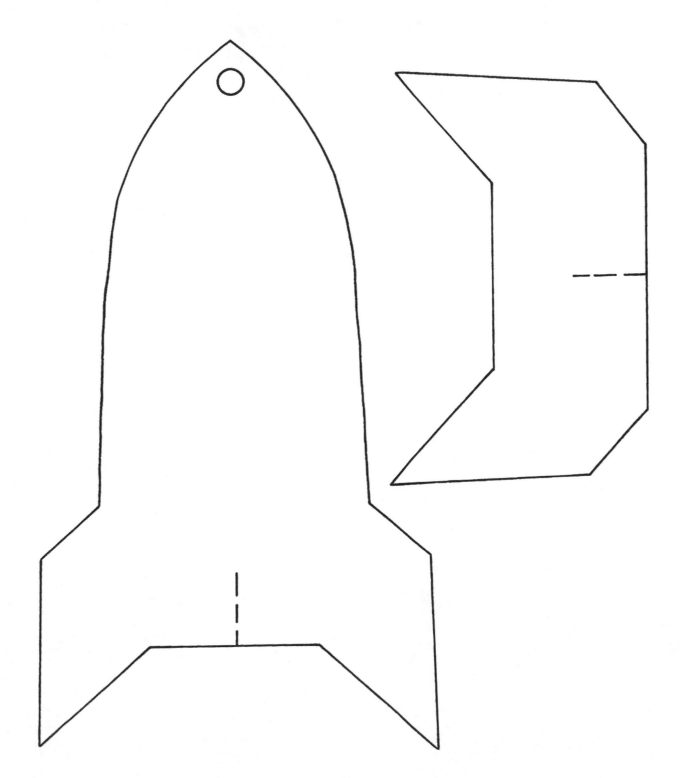